SALLY SCHNEIDER

Scrap Frenzy

Even More Quick-Pieced Scrap Quilts

Martingale™
& COMPANY

DEDICATION

For my first grandchild, Zachary Glen Schneider. The thrill of becoming your grandmother is more exciting than I ever imagined!

ACKNOWLEDGMENTS

No project of this magnitude is accomplished alone. Thank you to all the people who helped with this one. To my "Frenzied Friends," without whom this book would not have been possible. They suggested top-ten ideas, quilted quilts, and made quilts on very short deadlines. Each time a quilt arrived, it was like Christmas. You all did such an amazing job. Thank you from the bottom of my heart to Glenda Beasley, Sharyn Craig, Barb Eikmeier, Margie Fisher, Deb Moffett-Hall, Marion Harlan, Grace Jackson, Kari Lane, Dana Masera, Sue Phillips, Rita Powers, Judy Stephenson, Nancy Sweeny, Donna Thomas, and Cathie Yeakel.

To Judy Martin for permission to use the Bard of Avon block from *The Block Book*, © Judy Martin, 1998.

To Jane Townswick, who helped brainstorm the title for this third book in the series—she thought from happy to manic to frenzied was a logical progression.

To Gail Kessler and the Benartex fabric corporation, who provided some of the fabrics for these quilts.

To a good friend and great editor, Ursula Reikes, whose attention to detail caught all my mistakes.

Scrap Frenzy: Even More Quick-Pieced Scrap Quilts
© 2001 by Sally Schneider

That Patchwork Place® is an imprint of Martingale & Company™

Martingale & Company
20205 144th Ave. NE
Woodinville, WA 98072-8478
www.martingale-pub.com

Printed in Hong Kong
06 05 04 03 02 01   8 7 6 5 4 3 2 1

Library of Congress Cataloging-in-Publication Data

Schneider, Sally.

Scrap frenzy : even more quick-pieced scrap quilts / by Sally Schneider.

p. cm.

ISBN 1-56477-363-9

1. Patchwork—Patterns. 2. Quilting. 3. Patchwork quilts. I. Title.

TT835.S34697 2001

746.46'041—dc21

2001016270

MISSION STATEMENT

We are dedicated to providing quality products and service by working together to inspire creativity and to enrich the lives we touch.

CREDITS

President · Nancy J. Martin
CEO · Daniel J. Martin
Publisher · Jane Hamada
Editorial Director · Mary V. Green
Editorial Project Manger · Tina Cook
Technical Editor · Ursula Reikes
Copy Editor · Karen Koll
Design and Production Manager · Stan Green
Illustrator · Laurel Strand
Cover and Text Designer · Trina Stahl
Photographer · Brent Kane

Contents

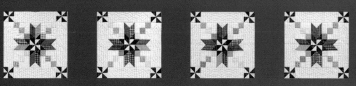

INTRODUCTION · 4

SCRAPS: HOW TO
GET THEM · 6

GREAT SCRAP QUILTS:
HOW TO MAKE THEM · 7

    Value · 7

    Variety · 8

    Pattern · 9

    Fabric Selections · 9

BASIC TECHNIQUES · 10

    Preparing Fabrics for Scrap Quilts · 10

    Sewing Accurate Seam Allowances · 11

    Making Strip Sets · 12

    Making Bias Squares · 12

    Making Quarter-Square Triangle Units · 14

    Sewing Folded Corners · 15

    Making Mary's Triangle Units · 15

QUILTS

    Album · 17

    Bard of Avon · 22

    Blackford's Beauty · 29

    Crazy Chain · 35

    Funky Chicken · 40

    Joseph's Coat · 46

    Magic Circle · 52

    Sunflowers/Morning Glories · 57

    Perkiomen Valley Nine Patch · 64

    Ray of Light · 68

    Skyrocket · 73

    Woven Star · 80

    Quartered Star · 86

QUILT ASSEMBLY AND
FINISHING · 90

    Quilts with Sashing · 90

    Diagonally Set Quilts · 91

    Borders with Straight-Cut Corners · 92

    Borders with Corner Squares · 92

    Quilt Backs · 93

    Basting · 93

    Binding · 94

    Labels · 95

ABOUT THE AUTHOR · 96

Introduction

I LOVE SCRAP QUILTS. For me, they are the most fun quilts to put together. Making a scrap quilt means that I get to play in my stash. I revisit old friends and discover some new ones. I get to find new, exciting color and print combinations. In short, I get to do what I love best—play with fabric. After making as many scrap quilts as I have, I find it extremely hard to make a quilt with just a few fabrics. I always want to throw in a few more pieces of this color or that or to add something I just found at the fabric store. Scrap quilts allow me to do whatever I want.

During the years I've been making scrap quilts, I have found that most people relate quickly to scrap quilts because they are the type of quilts our mothers or grandmothers made, and the type we grew up with. Non-quilters *especially* relate quickly to scrap quilts, and from non-quilters I've heard many heartwarming stories. Everyone seems to know someone who made a scrap quilt or has a scrap quilt, and has a story to tell about it.

I've made a lot of scrap quilts in the past fourteen years, and I have taught a lot of students what I know about these quilts. I've also learned a few things from both the quilts and the students in the process.

Probably the most important thing I've learned is that people are not very comfortable putting together fabrics that don't "go" together, especially when they are just starting to make scrap quilts. We are more comfortable making quilts the way we dress, with everything nicely coordinated and the colors and prints relating to one another. Many students bring similarly coordinated packets of fabrics to class to make their quilts, which is an easy way to start a scrap quilt. From them, I've learned that quilts in which each block is made from a different coordinated group of fabrics can be exciting and beautiful. Quite a few of the quilts in this book are made that way.

I've also learned that people often collect specific kinds of fabrics. These are the fabrics that they are drawn to, and although they don't have any special plans for using them, they keep collecting them. I've included several quilts made from these kinds of collections—plaids, novelties, period fabrics, batiks, florals, or even a collection of just one color.

The one thing I don't like about making traditional scrap quilts is having to cut all those pieces. Each time you use a fabric, you have to remove it from the shelf or drawer, press it, cut the required piece or pieces, and then refold the fabric and put it away. Either that, or you have to dump out a huge plastic bag or tub of scraps on the floor and sort through them all, choose your piece, cut what you need, and then bundle the whole thing back up. I'm not very likely to make a scrap quilt if that's how I have to do it. It's too much work. Besides, I've been using quick-piecing techniques to make my quilts for almost twenty years. I figured there had to be a way to combine fast techniques and scrappy-style quilts. So, I've developed a system of cutting fabrics ahead of time and storing them for the day I want to make a scrap quilt. You can read more about this system on page 10.

If you are starting your first scrap quilt and are not sure about cutting all the pieces at once, then you can cut them over time. Browse through the quilts in this book and choose one that appeals to you. Determine the size of the pieces required to make it, and start cutting those pieces from all the fabrics you purchase or pull from your stash for any

other reason. Keep the cut pieces together in a box or a bag, and before you know it, you'll have enough for your quilt.

Even if you are not planning a scrap quilt just yet, think about the fabrics you are using in the quilt you are working on right now. What might it look like if you added several more prints of the various colors you have chosen? Go back to the fabric store, get some more, and see what happens when you put them all together. I'd be willing to bet that you'll get a more exciting quilt than you would have with just a few fabrics.

WHEN YOU *prewash your fabrics, add a clean piece of muslin to the load. If fabric is going to run, it will run onto the muslin and you'll be able to see it easily. If the muslin comes out clean, chances are that the fabric, even though it might release dye into the water, will not run onto the other fabrics in your quilt.*

Scraps: HOW TO GET THEM

Here is my top-ten list of the best ways to acquire scraps for quilts.

1. Encourage your guild to play Quilt-O (bingo), with fat quarters as the price of each playing card and as the prizes for winning. Imagine my surprise when I won the "Blackout" game at a recent statewide quilt meeting—the prize was 144 fat quarters! I was in heaven.

2. Collect fat quarters. Wherever you go, purchase a few, either singly or in coordinated packets. Ask for fat quarters as gifts for all occasions (Valentine's Day, National Quilting Day, Mother's Day, and Halloween).

3. Organize a group within your quilt guild (no more than 8 to 10 people). Each month, bring a fat quarter to the "Queen for the Night." Take turns being queen.

4. Cut pieces from every fabric in your stash. Besides adding to your scrap pile, you will see what's really in that stash and find great fabrics you had forgotten you had. Just cut a few pieces each day until you get through the whole collection.

5. Cut up your spouse's old shirts, pajamas, and underwear. Will he really remember that his favorite shirt used to have long sleeves?

6. Subscribe to a mail-order fabric club. You'll get great additions to your stash—things you never would have purchased on your own.

7. Host a "Get Rid of Your Guilt" auction for your quilt guild. Bring in fabric that you know you'll never use and sell it. You'll get rid of things you don't like and pick up interesting things at a good price.

8. Beg a pregnant friend for her cotton maternity dresses (thanks to Barb, I'm still using pieces of her turquoise-print dress!).

9. Attend yard sales, especially in older neighborhoods.

10. Enter fat-quarter swaps on the Internet. Organizers usually advertise well in advance of the swap date, so you can shop sales to get your pieces.

Great Scrap Quilts:
HOW TO MAKE THEM

Over the fourteen years I've been making scrap quilts in earnest, I've made some good ones and some bad ones. I rejoice over the good ones, and I learn from the bad ones. They all have lessons to share.

VALUE

The first skill necessary to make a good scrap quilt is to know how to determine value and how to use it. Value is the relative darkness or lightness of a color.

To determine value, you need more than one piece of fabric. That's because value is relative—it depends on what other values are around it. A fat quarter may be light when you put it with fabric that is darker, but it becomes dark when you put it with fabric that is lighter.

The way I determine the value of my fabrics is to put everything I plan to use in a quilt on the floor: straight-grain strips, bias strips, and any other pieces I may cut into. I separate them into piles, one for each value required. Then I look at the piles carefully, checking to see that everything in one pile is a similar value, that nothing sticks out as being too different. I do this with each pile, checking also that nothing in the medium pile is darker than anything in the dark pile, and that nothing in the medium pile is lighter than anything in the light pile.

There are tools to help you determine value. If you have a red or green value viewer, you can hold that up to your eyes and look at the fabrics. The red or green removes color from the fabrics and leaves you with just light or dark. Remember, though, that value viewers distort the value of red and green fabrics. With the red viewer, red fabrics look very light, and green fabrics look dark. With the green viewer, greens look light and reds look dark. I tend not to use the value viewer very much, but some people really like it.

It helps to see the fabrics from a distance, but it's sometimes hard to get far enough away. That's when I get out my door peephole or binoculars. If you look through the wrong end of binoculars, they make things look far away; the peephole does the same thing. These are great tools for getting a better view of your fabrics and your projects.

You can get the same effect by looking at fabrics with barely-opened eyes. Squint at the piles. If you wear glasses to see at a distance, take them off; if you wear reading glasses, put them on. They all blur the lines of the prints and the colors somewhat, making it easier to notice if something stands out too much.

To best use value, determine which parts of a block are dark, which are medium, and which are light. Then, using your separated piles, make sure that the proper values are in the right place. You can see in the photographs of the traditional Barbara Frietchie Star below that the block is commonly constructed with two or three fabrics. The one on the left is made with three fabrics: one dark, one medium, and one light. The one on the right, however, was made with scraps. I've also used three values to make it—dark, medium, and light—but now, instead of just three fabrics, I've used thirty-two. The design is still the same, with the same values in the same places, but you've increased your fabric use by more than ten times.

A three-value block made with three fabrics

The same three-value block made with thirty-two fabrics

VARIETY

THE HALLMARK OF a scrap quilt is the large number and wide variety of fabrics used. In fact, the National Quilting Association doesn't consider a quilt in its scrap-quilt category unless it has at least seventy-five fabrics. I use all kinds of fabrics in my quilts, including plaids, prints, stripes, dots, florals, geometric prints, and novelty prints.

I especially like to use a few novelty or pictorial prints in each scrap quilt; it's fun to see this type of print in old quilts, and I want people to have the same enjoyment when they look at my quilts. My collection includes fabrics depicting bugs, candy bars, junk food, coffee, and computers. I have some great pieces with quilters' faces on them. One of the quilts in this book is composed of just novelty prints and a background (see "Memories" by Glenda Beasley on page 52).

The one type of fabric I don't use is solid-colored fabric. I feel that solids are eye-stoppers; because they stand out from the prints, they stop the movement of your eye around the quilt. besides, there are so many wonderful prints on the market these days that I prefer to use my money to purchase them. That doesn't mean that I don't use tone-on-tone prints. I use a lot of them. But a tone-on-tone fabric I choose usually has enough visual texture that it doesn't look like a solid color.

Choose a wide variety of colors and prints.

PATTERN

THE CONCEPT OF pattern in a scrap quilt is not easily defined. I usually call it a regular repetition of dark and light fabrics throughout the quilt that makes your eye move all around the piece. You don't get stuck somewhere because there are a lot of light or dark fabrics clustered in a particular spot. For example, in "Magic Circles in the Morning" on page 53, your eye keeps moving around each of the circular designs. The diagonal lines in "Crazy Chain" on page 35 are most obvious, allowing your eye to separate the star patterns. While it isn't necessary to use them, traditional patterns are a great source for scrap quilt designs.

My first scrap quilt was not successful and I almost quit making scrap quilts after that one. But as I looked at it and tried to figure out what was wrong with it, I realized that similar values were clustered together in sections, and there was no sign of a pattern. It was a valuable lesson. Sometimes you have to do something really wrong to learn how to do it right!

FABRIC SELECTIONS

THERE ARE SEVERAL methods I use to arrange fabrics to make successful scrap quilts.

Coordinated Blocks: For this method, choose one background for the whole quilt, then select a different coordinated group of fabrics (usually three or four) for each block. The resulting blocks are tied together with the common background fabric (which I usually use for sashing strips as well). These are the easiest kinds of scrap quilts to make if you are just starting out. Marion Harlon's "Stars in the Garden" (page 29) and both "Woven Star" quilts (pages 80 and 81) are excellent examples of coordinated blocks.

A variation of the coordinated method is called rainbow recipe, and is Donna Thomas's specialty.

She chose two colors for each block, one dark and one light, but used a different dark and light for each block. See her quilt "Jungle Stars" (page 87).

Color Menu: For this method, assign a specific color to each part of a block and make each block with that color selection. This method can be found in my quilt "Morning Glories" (page 58) and Nancy Sweeney's "Katie's Quilt" (page 57). The morning glories are various blue-and-yellow prints, while the sunflowers are yellow prints with sunflower-fabric centers. The leaves are made from an assortment of greens. Remember to use a large variety of each color, varying the prints in each block or each part of the block.

Mixing It Up: In this method, just pay attention to light and dark values and use all sorts of prints for the light and the dark, without regard to color or what "goes" with what. The resulting quilts always look wonderful, especially if you have followed the rules of value and pattern. Sharyn Craig's "Valley of the Scraps" (page 65), and Deb Moffett-Hall's "Daniel's Boon" (page 86) are good examples of mixing it up.

I like to use all the colors of the rainbow (and a few that you won't find there) in my quilts. But I work specifically to make sure that I use red and yellow whenever possible; those two colors really brighten up a scrap quilt. In the first scrap quilts I made, I wasn't particularly conscientious about using all the colors; I just used what I had in my stash, or what I felt like using. As I made more and more scrap quilts, I discovered that the more successful ones had red and yellow in them. Then I remembered something my mother told me when we were talking about gardens; she said that every garden needed some red and some yellow to bring it to life. I realized that the same thing was true with scrap quilts. I've also become enamored of lime green recently. I'd never wear that color, but I sure like what it does for my quilts.

Basic Techniques

PREPARING FABRICS FOR SCRAP QUILTS

ALL THE QUILTS in this book require one or more of six specific sizes of either strips or bias squares. As I looked at and analyzed traditional quilt patterns, I realized that many of them are made of squares and triangles. The most commonly used pieces in these patterns are 1½", 2", and 2½" straight-grain strips, and 2¼", 2⅝", and 3" bias strips. The bias strips are used to make 2", 2½", and 3" finished bias squares. These are the basic building blocks of all my scrap quilts. I also realized that by cutting and preparing these pieces ahead of time, I'd have a real head start on making scrap quilts.

I love to collect fat quarters, the 18" x 21" pieces of fabric that quilt shops often cut up and sell in coordinated bundles or place in pretty baskets so you can pick and choose what you want. I buy them wherever I go, and sometimes I buy lots of them. But often we get these pieces home and aren't sure what to do with them. I keep some on a shelf just to look at because the combination of colors and prints is so pretty, but eventually they all find their way into my scrap quilts.

From each fat quarter, I cut a 1½", 2", and 2½" straight-grain strip from the 21" width of the fat quarter. The remaining piece of fabric is about 10" x 21" after I trim the edge and square up the piece. From this strip, I cut bias strips as shown in the illustration. I do take care when cutting the bias strips to cut the light fabrics with the right side of the fabric up and the darker fabrics with the right side down. That way, when I pair dark and light bias strips to sew them together, they fit properly and I don't waste any fabric.

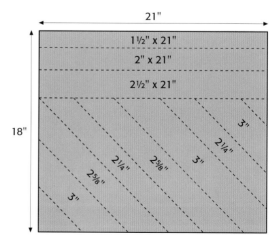

Pair the bias strips as described in "Making Bias Squares" on page 12, sew them together, and cut bias squares from them. I do this every day that I sew. Before I start in on my current project, I do about a half-dozen bias strips. It doesn't take much time, and it's a relatively painless way to acquire a good stash of different-size bias squares.

Store these strips, bias strips, and bias squares in plastic sweater boxes, separated by size only. (I tried storing them in shoe boxes when I started, but soon found that they were too small.) Use these boxes for leftover pieces from other quilt projects, too. Trim any bias squares to one of the three basic sizes; cut small amounts of leftover yardage into strips. Then when you want to make a Scrap Frenzy quilt, most of your cutting will be done. Just select the pieces you want to use and start sewing!

I have a rule about these scrap boxes. When they get full, I have to make a quilt. I never start collecting in a new box. I have two boxes for 1½" strips—one for dark ones and one for light ones—because I use a lot more of them than any other size. I have one box for each other size. There are so many great patterns out there that I want to make that it's not a problem to select a design and start sewing pieces together.

I don't limit myself, however, to using just fat quarters for scrap quilts. I often find patterns that require longer strips (such as Album and Woven Star). For these quilts, I select fabrics from my stash and cut pieces from the full width. I also cut short yardages (¼ yard or less) that I find on the shelf into strips and add them to my scrap boxes.

SEWING ACCURATE SEAM ALLOWANCES

THE MOST IMPORTANT skill for a quilter to master is making accurate ¼" seam allowances. We all think we can sew a ¼" seam, but it's not as easy

as it appears. You have to be only a little off to make a big difference in the way your pieces fit together. Even when I used my ¼" foot and an engraved line on my sewing machine at the ¼" mark, my pieces turn out too small. I had to find out where my own personal ¼" was on my machine.

Do the following test to make sure your seams are accurate. Cut 3 strips, each 2" x 6". Sew them together using your ¼" seam, and then press the seams to one side. Measure the strip set. It should be exactly 5" wide. If it's more or less than 5", even by just a little bit, your ¼" seam is not correct.

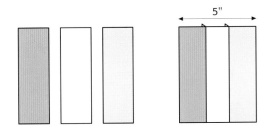

Repeat the sewing test, adjusting the seam allowance until you get it correct. When you do, take a file card or a small rectangle of template plastic and, with the sewing machine needle unthreaded, place the edge of the file card on your perfect ¼" mark; then stitch a line onto the file card or plastic. Now you have a record of your perfect ¼" on file, and you can always find it again. You can even change sewing machines and keep an accurate seam allowance. Just line up the stitched line with the machine's needle. The edge of the card is your perfect ¼" mark.

I stick a piece of moleskin on my machine to use as a stitching guide.

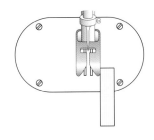

MAKING STRIP SETS

YOU CAN ASSEMBLE blocks or parts of blocks made with just squares and rectangles by cutting strips of fabric, sewing them together in a specific order to make a strip set, and then cutting the strip sets into segments. You'll use this method to make the Album pattern on page 7.

1. Sew strips together in the order required for your design. Press the seams toward the darker fabric. Use steam, but press carefully to avoid stretching. Press from the right side first, and then turn the unit over and press from the wrong side to be sure that all the seam allowances face in the proper direction.

2. Align a horizontal line of a small ruler with an internal seam of the strip set. Place the edge of your longer ruler along the left edge of the small one, then remove the small ruler and trim the uneven edge of the strip set. Cut segments from the strip set using the width specified in the quilt plan.

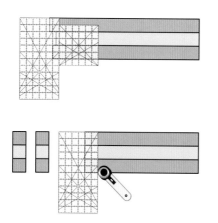

3. Join the segments to make the blocks or units required for your quilt.

MAKING BIAS SQUARES

THERE ARE PROBABLY as many ways to make bias squares as there are teachers. I've included two methods for making them. The following is an adaptation of a method developed by Sharyn Craig, and is my favorite.

1. Use the bias strips you cut when you prepare fat quarters for scrap quilts, or cut bias strips from yardage. Pair a dark and a light bias strip, right sides together. Sew along both long edges. Use a generous ¼"-wide seam. Press the stitched strips flat to set the seams.

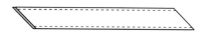

2. Place the bias strip unit on the cutting mat with the long point on the left side (on the right side if you are left-handed). Line up the diagonal line of a Bias Square® ruler with the left stitching line (right line for lefties) and trim away the excess fabric on the bottom of the strip.

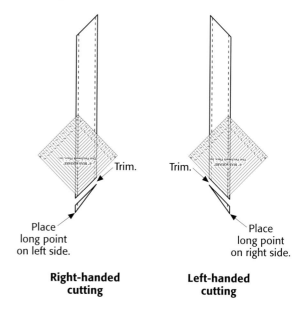

Place long point on left side. Trim.

Place long point on right side. Trim.

Right-handed cutting   **Left-handed cutting**

3. Move the Bias Square so that the diagonal line is on the seam and the desired cut size (from the chart on page 14) is on the trimmed edge. Cut along the edge of the Bias Square.

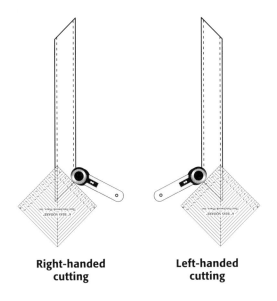

Right-handed cutting   **Left-handed cutting**

4. Turn the bias strip over and repeat step 3. Continue to flip and cut until you have reached the end of the bias strip unit. Press the seams toward the darker fabric and trim the "ears."

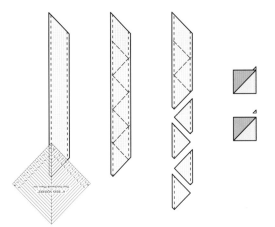

5. It is not usually necessary to trim the bias strip each time, but if you have made a miscut, you may need to trim again. If your seam allowance was not large enough, you may find a small square cut out of the corner of each bias square. If the square is smaller than ⅛", you can still use the bias square; the missing piece will be taken up in the seam allowance. To fix it on the rest of the strip, resew the bias strip with a wider seam allowance on one side. It is not necessary to rip out the old seam allowance. Occasionally, if your seam allowance was too wide, you may need to unpick a few stitches from the tip of the triangle. They usually come out easily when you open the bias square.

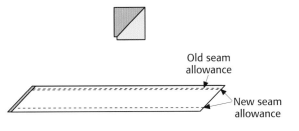

Old seam allowance

New seam allowance

To MAKE *it easier to find the cut-size line, place a stack (about 6 to 8) of sticky notes along the desired-size line on the underside of the ruler. Then place the diagonal line of the ruler on the seam, and slide the ruler up until the sticky notes bump the cut edge.*

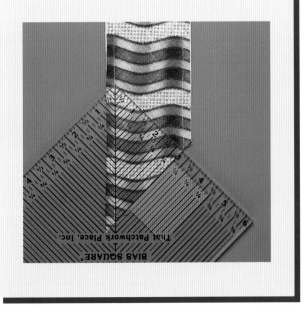

Strip Width for Bias Squares

Finished Size of Bias Square	Cut Width of Bias Strip	Cut Size of Bias Square
1½"	1⅞"	2"
2"	2¼"	2½"
2½"	2⅝"	3"
3"	3"	3½"
3½"	3⅜"	4"
4"	3¾"	4½"
4½"	4"	5"
5"	4⅜"	5½"

Strip Width for Quarter-Squares

Finished Size of Quarter-Square Triangle Units	Cut Width of Bias Strip	Cut Size of Bias Square
2"	2¼"	2⅞"
2½"	2⅞"	3⅜"
3"	3¼"	3⅞"
4"	3⅞"	4⅞"

Another method that is useful if you want only a few bias squares of two specific fabrics is to cut squares ⅞" larger than your desired finished size. Place the two squares right sides together; draw a line diagonally across the lighter square. Sew ¼" on each side of the line, then cut on the line. You will have two bias squares from each pair of squares.

1. Cut bias strips as indicated in the directions for the quilt you are making. Construct bias squares, following the directions on pages 12–13.

2. Place two bias squares right sides together, alternating the colors. Draw a line diagonally across the bias square, crossing the seam allowance. Sew ¼" from the line on both sides. Cut on the line, and press the seams toward one side.

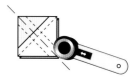

Use two colors to make these squares.

Use three colors to make these squares.

Use four colors to make these squares.

MAKING QUARTER-SQUARE TRIANGLE UNITS

TO MAKE QUARTER-square triangle units, start with bias squares. If you are using the bias strip method to make the bias squares, refer to the chart below to determine the correct size to cut the bias strips.

If you are cutting squares to make the bias squares, cut them 1¼" larger than the required finished size of the quarter-square triangle unit. Make the bias squares according to the directions above; then proceed to step 2.

SEWING FOLDED CORNERS

I LOVE THIS method for adding a triangle to the tip of a square or a rectangle, or for making flying-geese units and parallelograms. You need only squares and rectangles. The measuring is simple, as is the sewing. You don't even need to draw a sewing line. Although there is a little more fabric waste, the time and energy saved make it well worth it.

1. Place a piece of blue masking tape on your machine. I prefer blue tape because it shows up better on the machine. The right edge should be in a straight line from the needle toward you. Allow the tape to extend as far toward you as possible. If your machine is portable and you don't have a wide bed, attach the end of the tape to the table your machine sits on. Trim the tape away from the feed dogs.

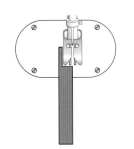

2. Place the small square on one corner of the large square, right sides together and raw edges even. Begin sewing exactly in the corner of the top square. As you stitch, keep the opposite corner directly on the edge of the masking tape.

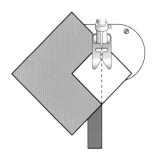

3. Trim the triangles ¼" from the seam; then press the triangle toward the corner.

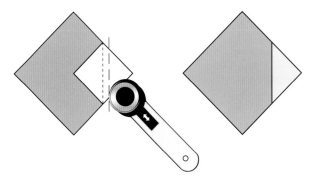

MAKING MARY'S TRIANGLE UNITS

THIS IS A little trick I developed years ago to quickly make Shaded Four Patch block units. It is named for my friend, Mary Kelleher, who was sitting next to me on the ski lift when I got the original idea.

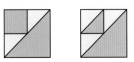

Mary's Triangle Units with squares and with triangles

1. Make bias squares or cut plain squares the required size.

2. Cut rectangles that are 1" longer than the square. If the square is 2" x 2", cut the rectangle 2" x 3".

3. Sew a rectangle to a square or bias square.

4. Sew pairs of pieced units together. In the center of each unit, clip the seam allowance through the seam line so that you can press the seams toward the rectangles.

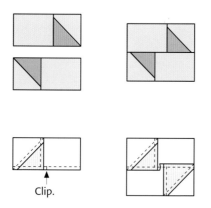

Clip.

5. Cut a square of template material equal to the short edge of the rectangle made in step 4. Cut the square in half diagonally. If the rectangle is 4" x 5", cut the square 4" x 4".

6. Place the template on the wrong side of each pieced rectangle, with the corner of the template on the plain square or bias square. Draw a diagonal line across the pieced rectangle unit. Repeat on the opposite corner of the pieced rectangle.

Template

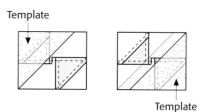

Template

Drawn lines

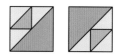

7. Place each pieced unit right sides together with a same-sized rectangle of another fabric. Sew on both lines, then cut between the lines. You may trim the seam allowance to ¼" if desired. Press the seams toward the larger triangle in each unit.

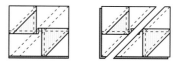

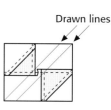

Beloved *by Sally Schneider, 2000, Breinigsville, Pennsylvania, 66½" x 66½". From the collection of Zachary Glen Schneider. I wanted to make a very special quilt for my first grandchild, and I thought the Album design with patches signed by the baby's parents, grandparents, and great-grandparents was pretty special. The collection of pastel colors matches the baby's nursery.*

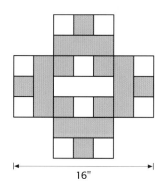

◄ ALBUM *by Rita Powers, 1999,*
Leavenworth, Kansas, 67" x 87½".
Rita's collection of country-style fabrics
were the perfect companion for the
floral-print background she chose for her quilt.

16"

MATERIALS

42"-wide fabric

	Crib	Twin	Queen
Finished Quilt Size	66½" x 66½"	66½" x 86½"	86½" x 106½"
Background	2⅜ yds.	3⅛ yds.	5⅜ yds.
Assorted Dark and Medium Prints	¼ yd. each of 13	¼ yd. each of 18	¼ yd. each of 32
Inner Border	½ yd.	⅝ yd.	¾ yd.
Outer Border	⅞ yd.	1 yd.	1¼ yds.
Backing	3½ yds.	5¼ yds.	7½ yds.
Batting	72" x 72"	72" x 92"	92" x 112"
Binding	½ yd.	⅝ yd.	¾ yd.

CUTTING FOR CRIB SIZE

	No. of Strips	Strip Width	No. of Pieces	Piece Size
Background	13	2½"	26	2½" x 11"
			13	2½" x 6"
			13	2½" x 6½"
	5	4½"	4	4½" x 14½"
			28	4½" x 4½"
	3	6½"	4	6½" x 10½"
			8	6½" x 6½"
Each Print	2	2½"	1	2½" x 11"
			2	2½" x 6"
			4	2½" x 6½"
Inner Border	6	2½"		
Outer Border	6	4½"		

CUTTING FOR TWIN SIZE

	No. of Strips	Strip Width	No. of Pieces	Piece Size
Background	18	2½"	36	2½" x 11"
			18	2½" x 6"
			18	2½" x 6½"
	6	4½"	4	4½" x 14½"
			40	4½" x 4½"
	4	6½"	6	6½" x 10½"
			11	6½" x 6½"
Each Print	2	2½"	1	2½" x 11"
			2	2½" x 6"
			4	2½" x 6½"
Inner Border	7	2½"		
Outer Border	7	4½"		

CUTTING FOR QUEEN SIZE

	No. of Strips	Strip Width	No. of Pieces	Piece Size
Background	32	2½"	64	2½" x 11"
			32	2½" x 6"
			32	2½" x 6½"
	11	4½"	6	4½" x 14½"
			68	4½" x 4½"
	7	6½"	8	6½" x 10½"
			23	6½" x 6½"
Each Print	2	2½"	1	2½" x 11"
			2	2½" x 6"
			4	2½" x 6½"
Inner Border	9	2½"		
Outer Border	9	4½"		

BLOCK ASSEMBLY

1. Sew two 2½" x 6" medium- or dark-print strips to a 2½" x 6" background strip. Make 1 set with each print. Crosscut each strip set into 2 segments, 2½" wide.

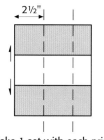

Make 1 set with each print.

2. Sew 2 segments from step 1 to opposite sides of a 2½" x 6½" background strip. Make 1 with each print.

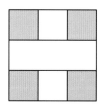

Make 1 unit with each print.

3. Sew one 2½" x 11" medium-or dark-print strip between two 2½" x 11" background strips. Make 1 set with each print. Crosscut each strip set into 4 segments, 2½" wide.

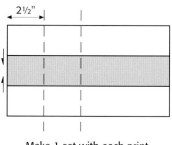

Make 1 set with each print.

4. Sew a segment from step 3 to a 2½" x 6½" medium- or dark-print strip. Make 4 with each print.

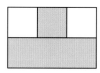

Make 4 units with each print.

QUILT ASSEMBLY AND FINISHING

1. Arrange and sew the pieced units and background pieces together as shown in the quilt plan for your size quilt. Be sure to keep matching units together.

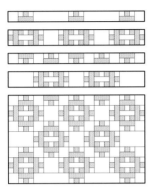

Crib

Twin

Queen

2. Referring to the directions for piecing, measuring, and adding borders on page 92, add the 2½"-wide inner border; then add the 4½"-wide outer border.

3. Layer the quilt top with backing and batting; baste.

4. Quilt as desired, or follow the quilting suggestion below.

5. Bind the edges and add a label.

CREATIVE OPTION

USE A FINE-POINT, permanent marking pen to write a name and date or favorite saying in the center rectangle of each Album block. Press a piece of freezer paper onto the wrong side of the rectangle to stabilize the fabric; remove the freezer paper after writing.

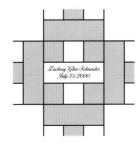

Bard of Avon

BARD OF AVON *by Grace Jackson, 2000, Puyallup, Washington, 44" x 64". Grace chose country-style prints for her version, making it a great comfort quilt. While she used the same fabric for all the small star (cornerstone) centers, she used different fabrics for the small star points. Block used with permission of Judy Martin.*

◄ BARD OF AVON *by Judy Stephenson,*
2000, Silverdale, Washington, 44" x 64".
Judy's selection of a dark background
makes the bright, jewel-tone fabrics sparkle. Her
value and fabric placement make the centers of
the stars look quite different from each other.
Block used with permission of Judy Martin.

Finished Block Size: 16"

MATERIALS

42"-wide fabric

	Lap	Twin	Queen
Finished Quilt Size	44½" x 64½"	64½" x 84½	84½" x 104½"
Background	2⅜ yds.	4¼ yds.	6¼ yds.
Assorted Dark Prints (2 per Block: Dark 1 and Dark 2)	1⅜ yds. total	2½ yds. total	3¾ yds. total
Assorted Medium Prints (2 per Block: Medium 1 and Medium 2)	¾ yd. total	1¼ yds. total	2 yds. total
Assorted Light Prints (2 per Block)	¾ yd. total	1¼ yds. total	2 yds. total
Backing	3 yds.	5¼ yds.	7¾ yds.
Batting	50" x 70"	70" x 90"	90" x 110"
Binding	½ yd.	⅝ yd.	¾ yd.

CUTTING FOR LAP SIZE

	No. of Strips	Strip Width	No. of Pieces	Piece Size
Background for Blocks	7	2½"	28	2½" x 2½" *
			38	2½" x 4½" **
	3	3⅜"	24	3⅜" x 4⅜"
Background for Sashing	3	16½"	17	4½" x 16½"
			10	2½" x 16½"
Assorted Dark Prints for Sashing	12	2½" x 20"	8 from each (96 total)	2½" x 2½"
	2	4½"	12	4½" x 4½"

CUTTING FOR TWIN SIZE

	No. of Strips	Strip Width	No. of Pieces	Piece Size
Background for Blocks	11	2½"	52	2½" x 2½" *
			66	2½" x 4½" **
	6	3⅜"	48	3⅜" x 4⅜"
Background for Sashing	5	16½"	31	4½" x 16½"
			14	2½" x 16½"
Assorted Dark Prints for Sashing	20	2½" x 20"	8 from each (160 total)	2½" x 2½"
	3	4½"	20	4½" x 4½"

* Reserve 4 squares for sashing cornerstones.
** Reserve pieces for sashing strips: Lap, 14; Twin, 18; Queen, 22.

CUTTING FOR QUEEN SIZE

	No. of Strips	Strip Width	No. of Pieces	Piece Size
Background for Blocks	17	2½"	84	2½" x 2½" *
			102	2½" x 4½" **
	9	3⅜"	80	3⅜" x 4⅜"
Background for Sashing	8	16½"	49	4½" x 16½"
			18	2½" x 16½"
Assorted Dark Prints for Sashing	30	2½" x 20"	8 from each (240 total)	2½" x 2½"
	4	4½"	30	4½" x 4½"

* Reserve 4 squares for sashing cornerstones.
** Reserve pieces for sashing strips: Lap, 14; Twin, 18; Queen, 22.

ADDITIONAL CUTTING

CUTTING DIRECTIONS ARE for 1 block. Repeat for the required number of blocks for your quilt. For each block, choose 2 dark prints, 2 medium prints, and 2 light prints that coordinate.

From one dark 1, cut:
* 1 strip, 2½" x 20". Crosscut the strip into 8 squares, 2½" x 2½".

From one dark 2, cut:
* 1 strip, 3¾" x 20". Crosscut the strip into 2 squares, 3¾" x 3¾", and 2 squares, 2⅞" x 2⅞".

From one medium 1, cut:
* 1 square, 4½" x 4½"

From one medium 2, cut:
* 1 strip 4⅞" x 20". Crosscut the strip into 4 squares, 4⅞" x 4⅞"; cut each square once diagonally.

From one light 1 fabric, cut:
* 1 strip, 3¾" x 20". From the strip, cut the following pieces:
  * 2 squares, 2⅞" x 2⅞"
  * 2 squares, 3¾" x 3¾"

From one light 2 fabric, cut:
* 1 strip, 2½" x 20". From the strip, cut the following pieces:
  * 4 rectangles, 2½" x 4½"
  * 4 squares, 2½" x 2½"

BLOCK ASSEMBLY

DIRECTIONS ARE FOR making 1 block. Repeat to make the required number of blocks for your quilt.

1. Place a 2⅞" light 1 square on top of a 2⅞" dark 2 square, right sides together. Draw a diagonal line on the back of the light square. Sew ¼" on each side of the diagonal line; cut on the drawn line. Repeat with another pair of squares to make a total of 4 bias squares.

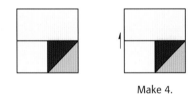

Make 2 pairs.

2. Sew 1 bias square from step 1, one 2½" background square, and one 2½" x 4½" background rectangle together to make a corner unit. Make 4 units.

Make 4.

3. Referring to "Sewing Folded Corners" on page 15, sew a 2½" dark 1 square to one end of a 2½" x 4½" light 2 rectangle. Trim; press toward the corner. Sew another 2½" dark 1 square to the opposite end of the light 2 rectangle with the seam going in the opposite direction to complete the star points. Trim and press. Make 4 star-points units.

Make 4.

4. Sew the star points, four 2½" light 2 squares, and one 4½" medium 1 square together to make the center star.

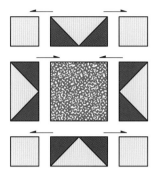

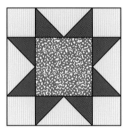

Make 1.

5. Repeat step 1, pairing 3¾" light 1 squares and 3¾" dark 2 squares to make 4 bias squares.

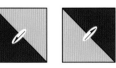

Make 2 pairs.

6. Sew a 3⅜" x 4⅜" background rectangle to a bias square from step 5. Repeat with the 3 remaining bias squares. Sew pairs of units together.

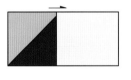

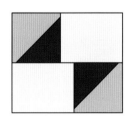

Make 2.

7. From template plastic, cut a 6½" square. Cut the square in half diagonally. Align the corner of the template with the pieced unit from step 6 and draw a line along the diagonal edge. Repeat on the opposite corner. Cut on the lines to make the edge triangles.

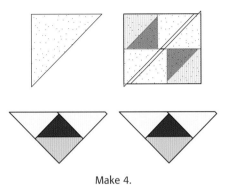

Make 4.

8. Sew two medium 2 triangles and an edge triangle together to make a side unit.

9. Referring to the illustration below, arrange and sew the units together into rows. Join the rows to complete the block.

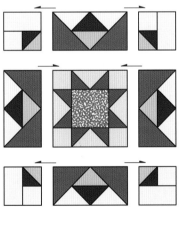

Lap: Make 6.
Twin: Make 12.
Queen: Make 20.

SASHING STRIPS ASSEMBLY

1. Using the folded corner technique, sew a 2½" dark square onto opposite corners of each 4½" x 16½" sashing strip. Sew a 2½" dark square to each remaining corner of the sashing strip.

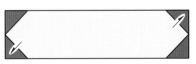

Lap: Make 17.
Twin: Make 31.
Queen: Make 49.

NOTE: *You can make the setting stars each from the same pair of fabrics (1 for the center and another for the points), or you can mix up the fabrics.*

2. Use the folded corner technique to sew a 2½" dark square on each end of the reserved 2½" x 4½" background rectangles to make the end pieces for the sashing strips. (These end pieces complete the stars).

Lap: Make 14.
Twin: Make 18.
Queen: Make 22.

QUILT ASSEMBLY AND FINISHING

1. Arrange the blocks, sashing strips, corner squares and end pieces as shown in the quilt plan for your size quilt.

2. Referring to "Quilts with Sashing" on page 90, sew the blocks and sashing strips together into rows. Stitch the sashing strips and cornerstones together into rows. Join the rows.

3. Layer the quilt top with backing and batting; baste.

4. Quilt as desired, or follow the quilting suggestion below.

5. Bind the edges and add a label.

Lap

Twin

Queen

Blackford's Beauty

STARS IN THE GARDEN *by Marion Shelton Harlan, 2000, Everett, Washington, 55" x 75". Quilted by Joanne Case. Marion loves pink-and-green and floral prints, and she was able to use her collection for her Blackford's Beauty quilt, including the wonderful rose border. She managed to make the whole quilt from her stash.*

◄ BLACKFORD'S BEAUTY IN PLAIDS
by Margie Fisher, 2000,
Thousand Oaks, California,
55" x 75". Quilted by Marilyn Petersen.
Margie has always loved plaids and has
quite a collection of them. For her
Blackford's Beauty, she used plaids for the light,
medium, and dark values, but she used a small
print for the background so she could keep
the values separate. She mixed up the fabrics in
each block, so her quilt has quite a
different look than Marion's.

Finished Block Size: 16"

MATERIALS
42"-wide fabric

	Lap	Twin	Queen
Finished Quilt Size	55½" x 75½"	75½" x 95½"	95½" x 95½"
Background	2¾ yds.	4¾ yds.	6½ yds.
2½" x 42" Light Prints	6	12	16
9" x 22" Medium Prints	6	12	16
9" x 22" Dark Prints	6	12	16
Inner Border	½ yd.	⅝ yd.	¾ yd.
Outer Border	1 yd.	1¼ yds.	1⅜ yds.
Backing	3½ yds.	5¾ yds.	8⅝ yds.
Batting	61" x 81"	81" x 101"	101" x 101"
Binding	½ yd.	⅝ yd.	¾ yd.

CUTTING FOR LAP SIZE

Cut all strips across the width of the fabric, except for bias strips. Cut bias strips with the right side up. See "Making Bias Squares" on page 12.

	No. of Strips	Strip Width	No. of Pieces	Piece Size
Background for Blocks	4	2½"	12	2½" x 12"
	3	4½"	6	4½" x 21"
	3	2½"	48	2½" x 2½"
	2	9"	12	2¼" bias strips *(cut with the right side up)*
Background for Sashing	2	16½"	17	4½" x 16½"
Inner Border	7	2"		
Outer Border	7	4½"		

CUTTING FOR TWIN SIZE

Cut all strips across the width of the fabric, except for bias strips. Cut bias strips with the right side up. See "Making Bias Squares" on page 12.

	No. of Strips	Strip Width	No. of Pieces	Piece Size
Background for Blocks	8	2½"	24	2½" x 12"
	6	4½"	12	4½" x 21"
	6	2½"	96	2½" x 2½"
	3	9"	24	2¼" bias strips *(cut with the right side up)*
Background for Sashing	4	16½"	31	4½" x 16½"
Inner Border	8	2"		
Outer Border	9	4½"		

CUTTING FOR QUEEN SIZE

CUT ALL STRIPS across the width of the fabric, except for bias strips. Cut bias strips with the right side up. See "Making Bias Squares" on page 12.

	No. of Strips	Strip Width	No. of Pieces	Piece Size
Background for Blocks	11	2½"	32	2½" x 12"
	8	4½"	16	4½" x 21"
	8	2½"	128	2½" x 2½"
	4	9"	32	2¼" bias strips *(cut with the right side up)*
Background for Sashing	5	16½"	40	4½" x 16½"
Inner Border	10	2"		
Outer Border	10	4½"		

ADDITIONAL CUTTING FROM ASSORTED PRINTS

From each 2½" x 42" light print, cut:
- 1 strip, 2½" x 12"
- 1 strip, 2½" x 21"

From each 9" x 22" medium print, cut:
- 1 strip, 6½" x 22". Crosscut the strip into 8 rectangles, 2½" x 6½".

From each 9" x 22" dark print, cut:*
- 2 bias strips, 2½" wide (cut with the wrong side up)
- 8 squares, 2½" x 2½"

* First cut the bias strips with wrong side up; then cut the squares from the leftovers.

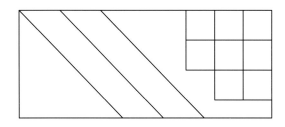

BLOCK ASSEMBLY

DIRECTIONS ARE FOR making 1 block. Repeat to make the required number of blocks for your quilt. For each block, choose 1 light, 1 medium, and 1 dark, or see "Creative Option" on page 34.

1. Sew a 2½" x 21" light strip to a 4½" x 21" background strip. Crosscut each strip unit into 8 segments, 2½" wide.

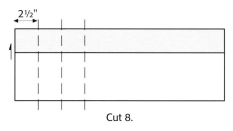

Cut 8.

2. Sew two 2½" x 12" background strips to a 2½" x 12" light strip. Crosscut each strip unit into 4 segments, 2½" wide.

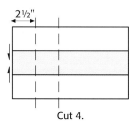

Cut 4.

3. Sew the segments together to complete a corner unit.

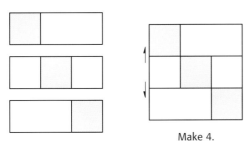

Make 4.

4. Referring to "Sewing Folded Corners" on page 15, sew a 2½" background square onto one end of each 2½" x 6½" medium rectangle. Sew 4 with seams facing one direction and 4 with seams in the opposite direction.

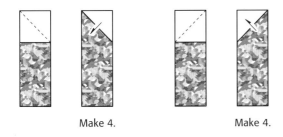

Make 4.   Make 4.

5. Repeat step 4 with dark squares on the opposite end of each rectangle. Stitch seams in the same direction as the background squares.

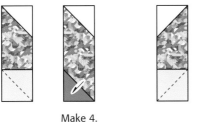

Make 4.   Make 4.

6. Sew the pieced rectangles together, matching the seams.

Make 4.

7. Referring to "Making Bias Squares" on page 12, sew a background bias strip to a dark bias strip along both long edges. Stitch 2 pairs of bias strips from each dark print. Cut 12 bias squares, 2½" x 2½", from each set.

8. Sew 4 bias squares together to form a pinwheel. Make 3 pinwheels; reserve 2 of them for quilt assembly. You will have pinwheels left over; save them for another project.

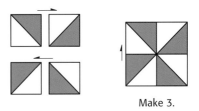

Make 3.

9. Arrange and sew the pieces together into rows. Join the rows to complete the block.

Lap: Make 6.
Twin: Make 12.
Queen: Make 16.

QUILT ASSEMBLY AND FINISHING

1. Arrange the blocks with the sashing strips and pinwheel corner squares as shown in the quilt plan for your size quilt. Referring to "Quilts with Sashing" on page 90, sew blocks, sashing strips, and corner squares together into rows; then join the rows.

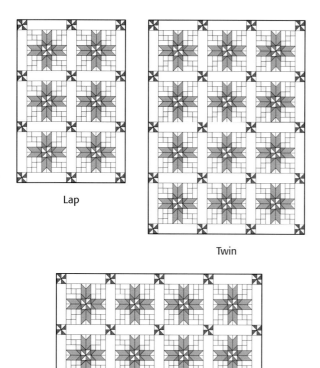

Lap

Twin

Queen

2. Referring to the directions for piecing, measuring, and adding borders on page 92, add the 2"-wide inner border; then add the 4½"-wide outer border. If you are using corner squares, measure and cut all 4 outer border strips at the same time. Cut 4½" squares of contrasting fabric and sew them to both ends of the shorter pieces; then add them to the quilt top.

3. Layer the quilt top with backing and batting; baste.

4. Quilt as desired, or follow the quilting suggestion below.

5. Bind the edges and add a label.

CREATIVE OPTION

INSTEAD OF USING just 1 dark, 1 medium, and 1 light in each block, mix up the fabrics so you have a variety in each block, like Margie Fisher did in her quilt on page 30. If you select this option, choose more fabrics of each value to give you more options for placement of the colors in each block. Cut the pieces for all the blocks before you select the pieces for each individual block.

Crazy Chain

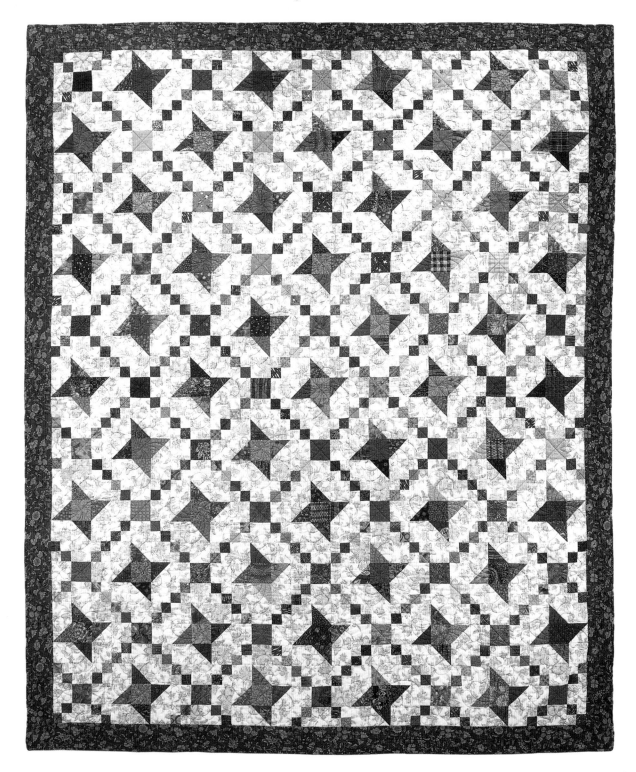

CRAZY CHAIN *by Sally Schneider, 2000, Breinigsville, Pennsylvania, 89" x 107". Quilted by Kari Lane. From the collection of Tyler and Amy McLaughlin. Several years ago, I moved my fabric from one part of the house to another with help from my son Ted. When we were finished, he announced that I couldn't buy any more blue fabric, since he had just moved about 24 cubic feet of blues. This quilt made almost no dent in that collection! The simple star block is a variation of Eccentric Star, and the alternate block forms a chain—an easy segue to the name "Crazy Chain."*

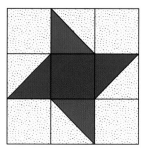 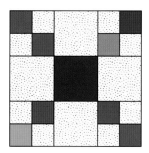

Finished Block Sizes: 9"

◄ BUFFET FOR BUNNIES *by Glenda Beasley, 2000,
Seoul, Korea, 92" x 110". Quilted by Jenny Moss.
When Glenda's mother-in law complained about rabbits
eating her flowers, Glenda vowed that when she had
a garden of her own, she would plant flowers for the
bunnies to eat. She did, and the bunnies had a feast.
She made this quilt to memorialize that experience.
Glenda participated in several Internet fabric swaps to get
all the floral fabrics she needed for this lovely, soft quilt.*

MATERIALS

42"-wide fabric

	Crib	Lap	Twin	Queen
Finished Quilt Size	40½" x 56½"	56½" x 74½"	74½" x 92½"	92½" x 110½"
Background	1¼ yds.	2¾ yds.	4½ yds.	6¾ yds.
3½" x 3½" squares Assorted Dark Fabrics	15	35	63	99
2" x 21" Strips Assorted Dark Fabrics	7	15	26	40
3" x 9" Bias Strips Assorted Dark Fabrics *	7	17	31	49
Inner Border	⅜ yd.	½ yd.	⅝ yd.	⅝ yd.
Outer Border	¾ yd.	⅞ yd.	1¼ yds.	1⅜ yds.
Backing	1¾ yds.	3 yds.	5¼ yds.	7½ yds.
Batting	46" x 62"	62" x 80"	80" x 98"	98" x 116"
Binding	½ yd.	⅝ yd.	¾ yd.	¾ yd.

* Cut bias strips with the wrong side up.

CUTTING FOR CRIB SIZE

Cut all strips across the width of the fabric, except for bias strips. Cut bias strips with the right side up. See "Making Bias Squares" on page 12.

	No. of Strips	Strip Width	No. of Pieces	Piece Size
Background	1	9"	7	3"-wide bias strips
	4	2"	8	2" x 21" *
	6	3½"	60	3½" x 3½"
Inner Border	5	2"		
Outer Border	5	4½"		

CUTTING FOR LAP SIZE

Cut all strips across the width of the fabric, except for bias strips. Cut bias strips with the right side up. See "Making Bias Squares" on page 12.

	No. of Strips	Strip Width	No. of Pieces	Piece Size
Background	3	9"	17	3"-wide bias strips
	8	2"	16	2" x 21" *
	13	3½"	140	3½" x 3½"
Inner Border	6	2"		
Outer Border	6	4½"		

CUTTING FOR TWIN SIZE

Cut all strips across the width of the fabric, except for bias strips. Cut bias strips with the right side up. See "Making Bias Squares" on page 12.

	No. of Strips	Strip Width	No. of Pieces	Piece Size
Background	5	9"	31	3"-wide bias strips
	13	2"	26	2" x 21"
	23	3½"	252	3½" x 3½"
Inner Border	8	2"		
Outer Border	8	4½"		

* You will have 1 extra strip.

CUTTING FOR QUEEN SIZE

CUT ALL STRIPS across the width of the fabric, except for bias strips. Cut bias strips with the right side up. See "Making Bias Squares" on page 12.

	No. of Strips	Strip Width	No. of Pieces	Piece Size
Background	7	9"	49	3"-wide bias strips
	20	2"	40	2" x 21"
	36	3½"	396	3½" x 3½"
Inner Border	9	2"		
Outer Border	9	4½"		

BLOCK ASSEMBLY

1. Referring to "Making Bias Squares" on page 12, sew each background bias strip to a dark bias strip along both long edges. Cut 4 bias squares, 3½" x 3½", from each set.

2. Sew 4 bias squares, four 3½" background squares, and one 3½" dark square together into rows. Join the rows to complete the block. You may make all 4 bias squares in a block from the same fabric or you may mix them up. (I prefer mixing them up!)

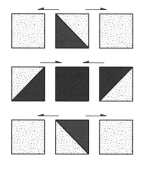
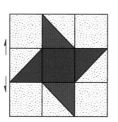

Crib: Make 7.
Lap: Make 17.
Twin: Make 31.
Queen: Make 49.

3. Sew each 2" x 21" dark strip to a 2" x 21" background strip. Crosscut the strip sets into 2"-wide segments as indicated. Sew pairs of units together, alternating dark and light squares.

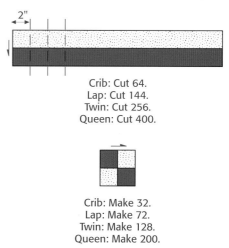

2"

Crib: Cut 64.
Lap: Cut 144.
Twin: Cut 256.
Queen: Cut 400.

Crib: Make 32.
Lap: Make 72.
Twin: Make 128.
Queen: Make 200.

4. Sew 4 four-patch units, four 3½" background squares, and one 3½" dark square together into rows. Join the rows to complete the block.

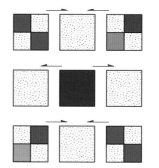
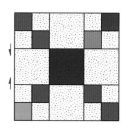

Crib: Make 8.
Lap: Make 18.
Twin: Make 32.
Queen: Make 50.

QUILT ASSEMBLY AND FINISHING

1. Arrange and sew alternating blocks together as shown in the quilt plan for your size quilt.

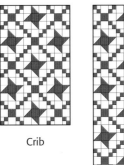

Crib

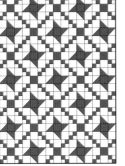

Lap

Twin

Queen

2. Referring to the directions for piecing, measuring, and adding borders on page 92, add the 2"-wide inner border; then add the 4½"-wide outer border.

3. Layer the quilt top with backing and batting; baste.

4. Quilt as desired, or follow the quilting suggestion below.

5. Bind the edges and add a label.

Funky Chicken

CHICKEN RUN *by Sally Schneider, 2000, Breinigsville, Pennsylvania, 50" x 50". A whole flock sits for a portrait in this more traditionally colored version of the Chicken block. I collected "chicken" prints for years before starting this quilt.*

◄ FUNKY CHICKEN *by Sally Schneider, 2000,*
Breinigsville, Pennsylvania, 18½ x 48½". I love chicken
quilts, especially appliqué quilts. I even purchased kits for a
block-of-the-month appliqué chicken quilt, even though
I don't appliqué! I thought there might be more people
who loved chickens and didn't appliqué, so I adapted
this old pattern and used my collection of "wild
and crazy" prints for the chickens.

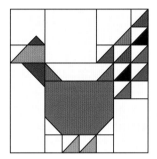

Finished Block Size: 12"

MATERIALS
42"-wide fabric

	Wall	Lap
Finished Quilt Size	18½" x 48½"	50½" x 50½"
Background	⅝ yd.	2½ yds.
Assorted Scraps (8 Fabrics per Chicken)	½ yd. total	⅞ yd. total
Assorted 1½" x 20" Strips for Sashing and Borders	24	32
Backing	1 yd.	3¼ yds.
Batting	24" x 54"	56" x 56"
Binding	⅜ yd.	½ yd.

CUTTING

<small>Cutting instructions are</small> for 1 block. Repeat for the required number of blocks for your quilt.

From background fabric, cut 1 strip 5" x 40" and 1 strip 2" x 40". (One 2" strip is enough for 2 blocks.)

	No. of Pieces	Piece Size
From the 5" strip, cut:	1	5" x 5"
	1	3½" x 5"
	1	3½" x 8"
	2	3½" x 3½"
	5	2⅜" x 2⅜"
From the 2" strip, cut:	1	2" x 6½"
	6	2" x 2"
For the chicken body, cut:	1	5" x 6½"
	1	2" x 2"
	1	2½" x 2½"
For the chicken feathers (1 each of 4 different fabrics), cut:	4	2⅜" x 2⅜"
	3	2" x 2" (1 for Prairie Point on head)
For the chicken head, cut:	1	2" x 3½"
For the chicken feet, cut:	1	2⅜" x 2⅜"

BLOCK ASSEMBLY

<small>Directions are for</small> making 1 block. Repeat to make the required number of blocks for your quilt. Refer to "Sewing Folded Corners" on page 15 for steps 1–5.

1. Sew a 2" background square on the 2 bottom corners of the 5" x 6½" chicken-body rectangle.

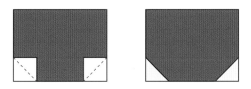

   <small>Note:</small> *The following directions are for a left-facing chicken. Directions for a right-facing chicken are in parentheses. See page 45 for a completed right-facing chicken.*

2. Sew a 2" chicken-body square on the left end of the 2" x 6½" background rectangle. Sew a 2" chicken-feather square on the other end.

3. Sew a 2½" chicken-body square on the top right corner of the 3½" x 8" background rectangle. (For a right-facing chicken, sew the square on the top left corner.)

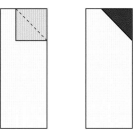

4. Sew a 2" background square on the upper left corner of the 2" x 3½" chicken-head rectangle. (For a right-facing chicken, sew the triangle on the top right corner.)

5. Sew a 2" chicken-feather square on one corner of a 3½" background square.

6. Place each of the 2⅜" background squares on top of a 2⅜" chicken-feather square or the chicken-foot square. Draw a line diagonally on the wrong side of the background square. Stitch ¼" from each side of the drawn line; cut on the line. Make a total of 10 bias squares (2 feet and 8 feathers).

7. Fold the 2" chicken-feather square in half diagonally; press the fold. Fold it again and press the fold. This Prairie Point forms the chicken's comb. Place the Prairie Point between the head section and the background piece above it, keeping raw edges even, before you stitch the seam.

8. Arrange and sew the pieced units and the background rectangles together to complete the Chicken block.

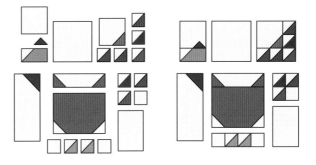

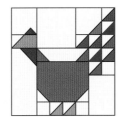

QUILT ASSEMBLY FOR THE LAP (NINE-BLOCK) QUILT

Cutting

From the assorted chicken fabrics, cut:
- 8 squares, 3" x 3"

From the background fabric, cut:
- 1 strip, 12½" x 42". Crosscut the strip into 12 pieces, 3" x 12½".
- 1 strip, 1¾" x 42". Crosscut the strip into 16 squares, 1¾" x 1¾".
- 5 strips, 2" x 42"

1. Using the folded corner technique, sew a 1¾" background square on each corner of 4 of the 3" chicken fabric squares to make the corner-stones.

2. Arrange and sew the blocks, background sashing strips, and cornerstones together as shown in the quilt plan for your size quilt. Refer to "Quilts with Sashing" on page 90.

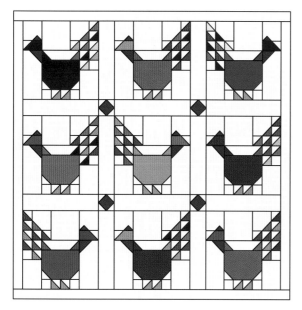

3. Referring to the directions for piecing, measuring, and adding borders on page 92, add the 2"-wide inner border.

4. To make the pieced outer border, sew 16 of the 1½"-wide strips together to make each of 2 strip sets. Crosscut each strip set into 6 segments, 3" wide.

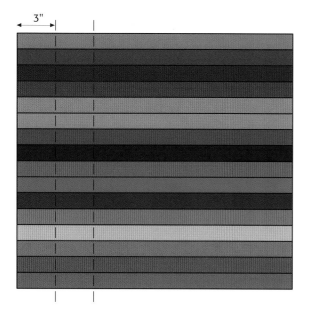

5. Join 3"-wide segments to make borders. Measure and trim them to the correct size. Sew the top and bottom borders to the quilt top. Sew the remaining 3" corner squares to each end of the side borders; then stitch the side borders to the quilt.

QUILT ASSEMBLY FOR THE WALL (THREE-BLOCK) QUILT

1. To make pieced sashing, sew the 1½"-wide strips together in groups of 6 strips. Make 4 strip sets. Crosscut each strip set into 6 segments, 3" wide.

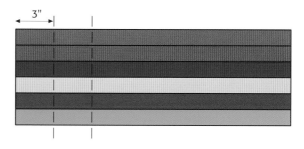

2. Join 2 segments to make each horizontal sashing strip and top and bottom border.

3. Sew the blocks with the sashing strips and top and bottom borders together.

4. Join 7 segments to make each of the side borders. Referring to the directions for piecing, measuring, and adding borders on page 92, measure and trim them to the correct size. From 1 chicken fabric, cut 4 squares, each 3" x 3", for the corner squares. Sew a square to each end of the side borders; then stitch them to the quilt.

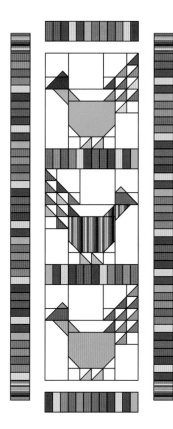

QUILT FINISHING

1. Layer the quilt top with backing and batting; baste.

2. Quilt as desired, or follow the quilting suggestion below.

3. Bind the edges and add a label.

Joseph's Coat

JOSEPH'S COAT *by Sally Schneider, 2000, Breinigsville, Pennsylvania, 60" x 77". Quilted by Kari Lane.*
A collection of Civil War–era reproduction fabrics and a photo of a quilt that I just had to make
were the starting places for this quilt.

◄ CHERRY, GRAPE, OR ORANGE *by Sally Schneider, 2000, Breinigsville, Pennsylvania, 43" x 60". I've been collecting batik fabrics for several years, but never had an opportunity to use them. I wondered how the Joseph's Coat pattern would look made exclusively with them. To me, it looks like a box of Popsicles!*

Finished Block Size: 14¼"

MATERIALS

42"-wide fabric

	Lap	Twin	Queen
Finished Quilt Size	43" x 60¼"	60¼" x 77½"	77½" x 94¾"
Assorted Dark Prints	1 yd. total	2¼ yds. total	2⅞ yds. total
Assorted Light Prints	1¼ yds. total	2¼ yds. total	3⅝ yds. total
Sashing and Border	1⅜ yds.	2⅛ yds.	3 yds.
Cornerstones	¼ yd.	¼ yd.	¼ yd.
Backing	2¾ yds.	3½ yds.	5½ yds.
Batting	49" x 66"	66" x 83"	83" x 101"
Binding	½ yd.	⅝ yd.	¾ yd.

CUTTING FOR LAP SIZE

From the assorted light prints, cut:
- 24 squares, each 2½" x 2½"
- 24 rectangles, each 2½" x 4½"
- 24 squares, each 3¼" x 3¼"
- 36 squares, each 3¾" x 3¾". Cut squares once diagonally for a total of 72 triangles.
- 6 squares, each 4⅛" x 4⅛". Cut squares twice diagonally for a total of 24 triangles.

From the assorted dark prints, cut:
- 6 squares, each 4½" x 4½"
- 48 squares, each 2½" x 2½"
- 72 squares, each 2⅞" x 2⅞". Cut squares once diagonally for a total of 144 triangles.

	No. of Strips	Strip Width	No. of Pieces	Piece Size
Sashing	1	14¾"	7	3½" x 14¾"
Cornerstones	1	3"	2	3½" x 3½"
Borders	5	6"		

CUTTING FOR TWIN SIZE

From the assorted light prints, cut:
- 48 squares, each 2½" x 2½"
- 48 rectangles, each 2½" x 4½"
- 48 squares, each 3¼" x 3¼"
- 72 squares, each 3¾" x 3¾". Cut squares once diagonally for a total of 144 triangles.
- 12 squares, each 4⅛" x 4⅛". Cut squares twice diagonally for a total of 48 triangles.

From the assorted dark prints, cut:
- 12 squares, each 4½" x 4½"
- 96 squares, each 2½" x 2½"
- 144 squares, each 2⅞" x 2⅞". Cut squares once diagonally for a total of 288 triangles.

	No. of Strips	Strip Width	No. of Pieces	Piece Size
Sashing	2	14¾"	17	3½" x 14¾"
Cornerstones	1	3"	6	3½" x 3½"
Borders	7	6"		

CUTTING FOR QUEEN SIZE

From the assorted light prints, cut:

- 80 squares, each 2½" x 2½"
- 80 rectangles, each 2½" x 4½"
- 80 squares each 3¼" x 3¼"
- 120 squares, each 3¾" x 3¾". Cut squares once diagonally for a total of 240 triangles.
- 20 squares, each 4⅛" x 4⅛". Cut squares twice diagonally for a total of 80 triangles.

From the assorted dark prints, cut:

- 20 squares, each 4½" x 4½"
- 160 squares, each 2½" x 2½"
- 240 squares, each 2⅞" x 2⅞". Cut squares once diagonally for a total of 480 triangles.

	No. of Strips	Strip Width	No. of Pieces	Piece Size
Sashing	3	14¾"	31	3½" x 14¾"
Cornerstones	2	3½"	12	3½" x 3½"
Borders	9	6"		

BLOCK ASSEMBLY

DIRECTIONS ARE FOR making 1 block. Repeat to make the required number of blocks for your quilt.

1. Referring to "Sewing Folded Corners" on page 15, sew a 2½" dark square onto one end of a 2½" x 4½" light rectangle. Trim and press. Sew another 2½" dark square onto the opposite end of the light rectangle. Trim and press.

Make 4.

2. Sew 4 pieced units from step 1, four 2½" light squares, and one 4½" dark square together to make the center star.

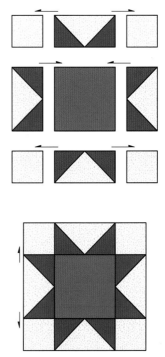

Make 1.

3. Sew 4 dark triangles to the sides of a 3¼" light square.

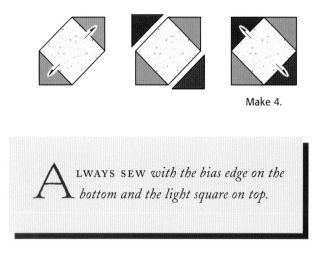

Make 4.

> ALWAYS SEW *with the bias edge on the bottom and the light square on top.*

4. Sew 2 light half-square triangles to opposite sides of each unit from step 3. Then sew another triangle to one side.

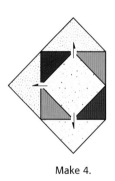

Make 4.

5. Sew 2 dark triangles to the sides of the pieced units from step 4. Add 2 light quarter-square triangles to 2 of the pieced units.

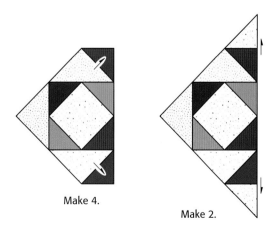

Make 4.

Make 2.

6. Arrange and sew the pieced units together to complete the block.

Lap: Make 6.
Twin: Make 12.
Queen: Make 20.

QUILT ASSEMBLY AND FINISHING

1. Arrange and sew the blocks and sashing strips together as shown in the quilt plan for your size quilt. Refer to "Quilts with Sashing" on page 90.

Lap

Twin

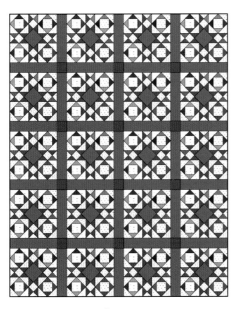

Queen

2. Referring to the directions for piecing, measuring, and adding borders on page 92, add the 6"-wide border.

3. Layer the quilt top with backing and batting; baste.

4. Quilt as desired, or follow the quilting suggestion below.

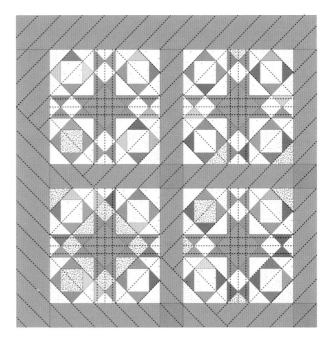

5. Bind the edges and add a label.

Magic Circle

MEMORIES *by Glenda Beasley, 2000, Seoul, South Korea, 46½" x 58½". Quilted by Jenny Moss. Glenda used a wide selection of novelty prints for her quilt, selecting those that had specific meaning for her. Some of the prints came from Internet fabric swaps. She worked hard to make sure that all the directional fabrics ended up facing the right direction.*

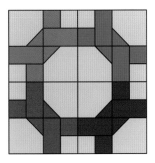

◄ MAGIC CIRCLES IN THE MORNING
by Cathie Yeakel, 2000, Quakertown,
Pennsylvania, 82" x 94".
Cathie has a full-time job and a family, but
manages to make lots of quilts by getting up
early to sew. She pieced the quilt top in a month
of mornings and quilted it the same way. She
got creative with the pattern and cut up some of
the 4" sample squares she received in the mail
for this quilt.

Finished Block Size: 12"

MATERIALS

42"-wide fabric

	Lap	Twin	Queen
Finished Quilt Size	46½" x 58½"	58½" x 82½"	82½" x 94½"
Background	1⅜ yds.	2¾ yds.	4¾ yds.
2" x 18" Dark Strips	48	96	168
Inner Border	⅜ yd.	½ yd.	½ yd.
Outer Border	¾ yd.	1⅛ yds.	1¼ yds.
Backing	3 yds.	5 yds.	7½ yds.
Batting	52" x 64"	64" x 88"	88" x 100"
Binding	½ yd.	⅝ yd.	¾ yd.

CUTTING FOR LAP SIZE

	No. of Strips	Strip Width	No. of Pieces	Piece Size
Background	5	2"	96	2" x 2"
	9	3½"	96	3½" x 3½"
Each Dark Strip	1	2" x 18"	4	2" x 2"
			2	2" x 3½"
Inner Border	5	1½"		
Outer Border	5	4½"		

CUTTING FOR TWIN SIZE

	No. of Strips	Strip Width	No. of Pieces	Piece Size
Background	10	2"	192	2" x 2"
	18	3½"	192	3½" x 3½"
Each Dark Strip	1	2" x 18"	4	2" x 2"
			2	2" x 3½"
Inner Border	8	1½"		
Outer Border	8	4½"		

CUTTING FOR QUEEN SIZE

	No. of Strips	Strip Width	No. of Pieces	Piece Size
Background	17	2"	336	2" x 2"
	31	3½"	336	3½" x 3½"
Each Dark Strip	1	2" x 18"	4	2" x 2"
			2	2" x 3½"
Inner Border	9	1½"		
Outer Border	9	4½"		

BLOCK ASSEMBLY

1. Sew a 2" dark square to a 2" background square. Make 2 units with matching dark squares. Add a 2" x 3½" matching dark rectangle to each pair of squares.

Make 2.

2. Referring to "Sewing Folded Corners" on page 15, sew a 2" dark square (to match the units made in step 1) to one corner of each of two 3½" background squares.

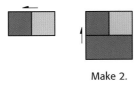

Make 2.

3. Sew 2 units from step 1 and 2 units from step 2 together to make a quarter block. Repeat with all dark fabrics.

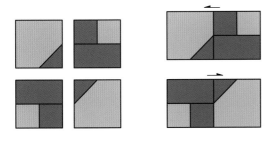

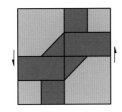

4. Sew 4 quarters together to complete the block.

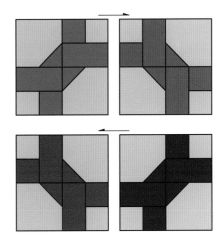

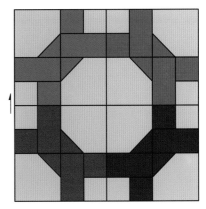

Lap: Make 12.
Twin: Make 24.
Queen: Make 42.

QUILT ASSEMBLY AND FINISHING

1. Arrange and sew the blocks together as shown in the quilt plan for your size quilt.

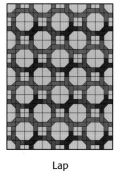

Lap

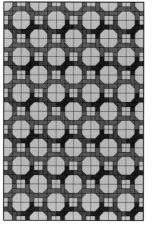

Twin

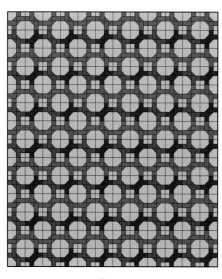

Queen

2. Referring to the directions for piecing, measuring, and adding borders on page 92, add the 1½"-wide inner border, then the 4½"-wide outer border.

3. Layer the quilt top with backing and batting; baste.

4. Quilt as desired, or follow the quilting suggestion below.

5. Bind the edges and add a label.

CREATIVE OPTION

CATHIE YEAKEL'S QUILT, "Magic Circles in the Morning" (page 53), is made using 2 different fabrics in each quarter unit. If you get packages of 4" or 6" squares in the mail, use them to make this quilt. Two 4" or 6" squares will yield enough pieces for 1 quarter unit. From each square, cut 2 squares, each 2" x 2", and 1 rectangle, 2" x 3½". Make 2 four-patch units and 2 folded-corner units for each quarter unit. Sew 4 quarter units together to make 1 block.

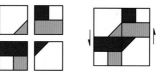

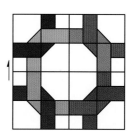

Sunflowers/Morning Glories

KATIE'S QUILT *by Nancy Sweeny, 2000, Arlington, Washington, 44½" x 61½". Quilted by Kathy Davenport.*
Nancy's great collection of yellow fabrics and sunflower prints, all on a clear, sky blue background, makes you feel like you can just reach out and touch the flowers.

MORNING GLORIES *by Sally Schneider, 2000, Breinigsville, Pennsylvania, 28" x 62". From the time I started gardening, I've always grown morning glories. Seeing their cheerful faces early every morning starts my day off the right way. Still no noticeable dent in my collection of blue fabrics!*

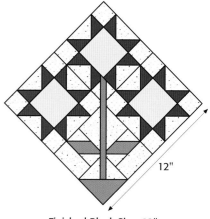

Finished Block Size: 12"

MATERIALS
42"-wide fabric

	Wall	Lap	Twin	Queen
Finished Quilt Size	27½" x 61½"	44½" x 61½"	61½" x 78½"	78½" x 95½"
Background	1½ yds.	2¼ yds.	4¼ yds.	6¼ yds.
Flower Petal Prints 2" x 18" Strips	9	24	54	96
Optional Flower Accent 2" x 9" Strips	9	24	54	96
Flower Center Prints 3½" x 3½" Squares	9	24	54	96
Leaf and Stem Prints 3½" x 20" Strips	3	8	18	32
Inner Border	⅜ yd.	⅜ yd.	½ yd.	½ yd.
Outer Border	¾ yd.	¾ yd.	1¼ yds.	1⅜ yds.
Optional Fabric for Piping	⅜ yd.	⅜ yd.	½ yd.	½ yd.
Backing	2 yds.	3 yds.	4 yds.	6 yds.
Batting	33" x 67"	50" x 67"	67" x 84"	84" x 101"
Binding	½ yd.	½ yd.	⅝ yd.	¾ yd.

CUTTING FOR WALL SIZE

	No. of Strips	Strip Width	No. of Pieces	Piece Size
Background	7	2"	42	2" x 3½"
			48	2" x 2"
	1	3½"	6	3½" x 3½"
	1	19"	1	19" x 19" ⊠ *
	1	10"	2	10" x 10" ◻ **
Inner Border	5	1½"		
Outer Border	5	4½"		
Optional Piping	5	1¾"		

CUTTING FOR LAP SIZE

	No. of Strips	Strip Width	No. of Pieces	Piece Size
Background	18	2"	112	2" x 3½"
			128	2" x 2"
	2	3½"	16	3½" x 3½"
	1	19"	2	19" x 19" ⊠ *
	1	10"	2	10" x 10" ◻ **
Inner Border	5	1½"		
Outer Border	5	4½"		
Optional Piping	5	1¾"		

CUTTING FOR TWIN SIZE

	No. of Strips	Strip Width	No. of Pieces	Piece Size
Background	38	2"	252	2" x 3½"
			288	2" x 2"
	4	3½"	36	3½" x 3½"
	2	19"	3	19" x 19" ⊠ *
	1	10"	2	10" x 10" ◻ **
Inner Border	7	1½"		
Outer Border	7	4½"		
Optional Piping	7	1¾"		

* Cut each square twice diagonally for side-setting triangles.
** Cut each square once diagonally for corner-setting triangles..

CUTTING FOR QUEEN SIZE

	No. of Strips	Strip Width	No. of Pieces	Piece Size
Background	67	2"	448	2" x 3½"
			512	2" x 2"
	6	3½"	64	3½" x 3½"
	2	19"	4	19" x 19" ⊠ *
	1	10"	2	10" x 10" ◺ **
Inner Border	9	1½"		
Outer Border	9	4½"		
Optional Piping	9	1¾"		

* Cut each square twice diagonally for side-setting triangles.
** Cut each square once diagonally for corner-setting triangles..

CUTTING FOR FLOWERS AND LEAVES

CUTTING INSTRUCTIONS ARE for 1 block. Repeat for the required number of blocks for your quilt.

From each of 3 flower-petal prints, cut:
- 8 squares, each 2" x 2" (24 total)

(Optional) From each of 3 flower-accent strips, cut
- 4 squares, each 2" x 2" (12 total)

From each of 3 flower-center prints, cut:
- 1 square, 3½" x 3½" (3 total)

From 1 leaf print, cut:
- 2 rectangles, each 2" x 3½"
- 1 square, 3½" x 3½"
- 1 strip, 1" x 12½"

BLOCK ASSEMBLY

DIRECTIONS ARE FOR making 1 block. Repeat to make the required number of blocks for your quilt.

1. Referring to "Sewing Folded Corners" on page 15, sew a 2" flower petal square on each end of a 2" x 3½" background rectangle. If you choose the optional flower accent, sew a 2" accent square on each corner of a 3½" flower center.

Make 3 sets of 4.

Optional: Make 3 for each block.

2. Sew 4 pieced petal units, one 3½" flower center, and four 2" background squares to complete the flower.

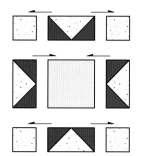 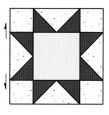

Make 2.

3. For the stem, fold under ¼" on each long edge of the 1" x 12½" leaf-print strip.

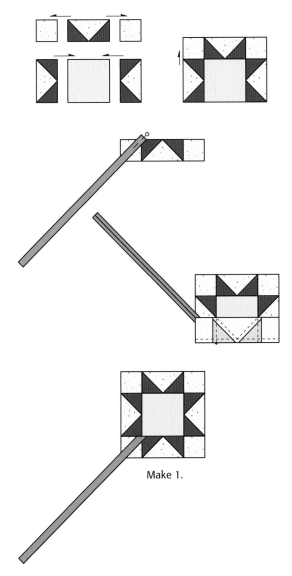

Make 1.

4. Arrange the pieces as you did in step 2. Sew the units together into rows. Sew the first 2 rows together. Place the stem piece diagonally across the background square on the last row of the block, making sure it is centered on the square. The raw edges should extend beyond the seam allowance. Pin the stem in place, then pin this row to the first 2 rows of the block, matching the seams. Sew the rows together. You will stitch the remainder of the stem later.

Make 1.

5. For the leaves, sew a 2" background square on each end of a 2" x 3½" leaf-print rectangle using the folded corner technique. Sew both seams on a leaf-print rectangle in the same direction, but sew the seams on the 2 leaves in opposite directions.

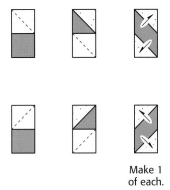

Make 1
of each.

6. Sew the 2 units from step 5, two 2" x 3½" background rectangles, and two 3½" background squares together to make the leaf unit.

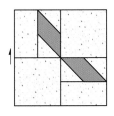

Make 1.

7. Sew together 3 flower units and 1 leaf unit as shown, keeping the stem free. Fold the stem diagonally across the leaf unit and stitch it to the block along both edges of the stem. You can stitch it by hand or machine. Trim the edges of the stem even with the block.

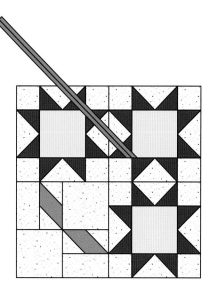

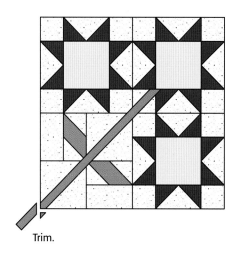

Trim.

8. Using the folded corner technique, sew a 3½" leaf-print square on the stem corner of the block; use a square to match the stem fabric. Trim and press.

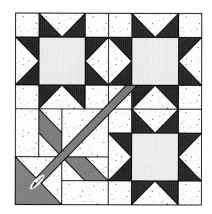

Wall: Make 3.
Lap: Make 8.
Twin: Make 18.
Queen: Make 32.

QUILT ASSEMBLY AND FINISHING

1. Referring to "Diagonally Set Quilts" on page 91, arrange and sew the blocks and side-setting triangles together into diagonal rows as shown in the quilt plan for your size quilt. Join the rows, adding the corner triangles last. Trim the edges of the quilt before adding borders.

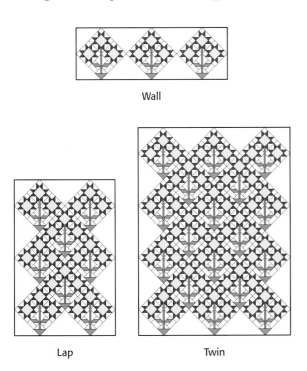

Wall

Lap

Twin

Queen

2. Referring to the directions for piecing, measuring, and adding borders on page 92, add the 1½"-wide inner border, then the 4½"-wide outer border. If you choose the piping option, stitch the piping strips together to make them long enough for the sides of the quilt. Fold the strips in half, wrong sides together. Press, then pin or baste them to the edges of the inner border strip before you add the outer border.

3. Layer the quilt top with backing and batting; baste.

4. Quilt as desired, or follow the quilting suggestion below.

5. Bind the edges and add a label.

Perkiomen Valley Nine Patch

PERKIOMEN VALLEY IN THE 1930S *by Susan Phillips, 2000, Fairbanks, Alaska, 70" x 70".*
Sue loves Nine Patch block variations, and she has been collecting fat quarters and fat eighths of 1930s reproduction fabrics
since she has been quilting. This design was a perfect marriage of interests.

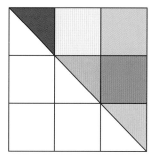

◀ VALLEY OF THE SCRAPS
by Sharyn Craig, 2000, El Cajon, California, 45" x 45". Sharyn has a prodigious collection of fabrics, and she drew from the whole collection to make this crib-sized version of the Perkiomen Valley pattern. She chose red and all its variations, from red-orange to burgundy to purple, for the dark triangles in each block.

Finished Block Size:
6" (crib and twin)
7½" (queen)

MATERIALS
42"-wide fabric

	Crib	Twin	Queen
Finished Quilt Size	44½" x 44½"	70½" x 70½"	85½" x 85½"
2½" x 21" Light Strips	14	38	
2½" x 21" Dark Strips	14	38	
2" Finished Bias Squares *	108	300	
3" x 21" Light Strips			50
3" x 21" Dark Strips			50
2½" Finished Bias Squares *			300
Inner Border	¼ yd.	⅝ yd.	⅝ yd.
Outer Border	½ yd.	1⅛ yds.	1¼ yds.
Backing	3 yds.	4½ yds.	7½ yds.
Batting	50" x 50"	76" x 76"	91" x 91"
Binding	⅜ yd.	⅝ yd.	¾ yd.

* Use bias squares from your stash or use your favorite method to make the required number. See "Making Bias Squares" on page 12. For 2" finished bias squares, cut bias squares 2½" x 2½"; for 2½" finished bias squares, cut bias squares 3" x 3".

CUTTING BORDERS FOR CRIB SIZE

	No. of Strips	Strip Width
Inner Border	4	1½"
Outer Border	5	3½"

CUTTING BORDERS FOR TWIN SIZE

	No. of Strips	Strip Width
Inner Border	8	1½"
Outer Border	8	4½"

CUTTING BORDERS FOR QUEEN SIZE

	No. of Strips	Strip Width
Inner Border	8	1½"
Outer Border	9	4½"

BLOCK ASSEMBLY

1. Cut the 2½"-wide light and dark strips into 2½" squares; cut a total of 108 light and 108 dark squares for the crib size, 300 light and 300 dark squares for the twin size. For the queen size, cut the 3"-wide light and dark strips into 3" squares; cut 300.

2. Sew together 3 light squares, 3 dark squares, and 3 bias squares (2½" cut for crib or twin; 3" cut for queen) to complete the block.

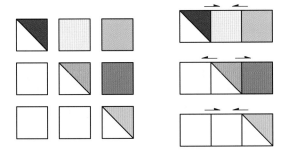

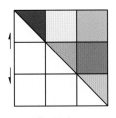

Crib: Make 36.
Twin and queen: Make 100.

QUILT ASSEMBLY AND FINISHING

1. Arrange and sew the blocks together as shown in the quilt plan for your size quilt.

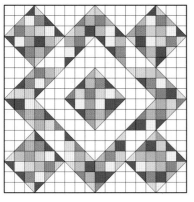

Crib

Twin/Queen

2. Referring to the directions for piecing, measuring, and adding borders on page 92, add the 1½"-wide inner border; then add the 3½"- or 4½"-wide outer border.

3. Layer the quilt top with backing and batting; baste.

4. Quilt as desired, or follow the quilting suggestion below.

5. Bind the edges and add a label.

Ray of Light

RAY OF LIGHT *by Sally Schneider, 1999, Breinigsville, Pennsylvania, 44" x 61". The block,*
designed to be made with Mary's Triangles units, was the starting place for this quilt.
It is named "Ray of Light" because that is the translation of the first name of its recipient, Rashmi Kharbanda.
It is made in blues, yellows, and reds because those are her favorite colors.

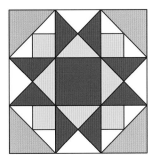

◄ HOLIDAY FRENZY *by Barbara J. Eikmeier,
2000, Seoul, South Korea, 42" x 59". Barb made all the
parts to the blocks and laid them out like the directions
said. Suddenly a frenzy began in the sewing room. It
resulted in the pieces getting mixed up before the blocks
were sewn together. Each block ended up with two reds
and two greens, making the stars appear more scrappy.
That's from someone who says she doesn't like making
scrap quilts. This kind, she likes!*

Finished Block Size: 12"

MATERIALS
42"-wide fabric

	Lap	Twin	Queen
Finished Quilt Size	44½" x 61½"	61½" x 78½"	78½" x 95½"
Background	⅝ yd.	1¼ yds.	1¾ yds.
6" x 18" Dark Strips	8	18	32
6" x 18" Medium 1 Strips	4	9	18
6" x 18" Medium 2 Strips	4	9	18
Setting Triangles	1 yd.	1½ yds.	1½ yds.
Inner Border	⅜ yd.	½ yd.	½ yd.
Outer Border	¾ yd.	1 yd.	1¼ yds.
Backing	3 yds.	4 yds.	6 yds.
Batting	50" x 67"	67" x 84"	84" x 101"
Binding	½ yd.	⅝ yd.	¾ yd.

CUTTING FOR LAP SIZE

	No. of Strips	Strip Width	No. of Pieces	Piece Size
Background	2	3½"	32	2½" x 3½"
	2	5¼"	8	5¼" x 5¼"
Setting Triangles	1	19"	2	19" x 19" ⊠ *
	1	10"	2	10" x 10" ◩ **
Inner Border	5	1½"		
Outer Border	5	4½"		

CUTTING FOR TWIN SIZE

	No. of Strips	Strip Width	No. of Pieces	Piece Size
Background	5	3½"	72	2½" x 3½"
	3	5¼"	18	5¼" x 5¼"
Setting Triangles	2	19"	3	19" x 19" ⊠ *
	1	10"	2	10" x 10" ◩ **
Inner Border	7	1½"		
Outer Border	7	4½"		

CUTTING FOR QUEEN SIZE

	No. of Strips	Strip Width	No. of Pieces	Piece Size
Background	8	3½"	128	2½" x 3½"
	5	5¼"	32	5¼" x 5¼"
Setting Triangles	2	19"	4	19" x 19" ⊠ *
	1	10"	2	10" x 10" ◩ **
Inner Border	9	1½"		
Outer Border	9	4½"		

* Cut each square twice diagonally for side-setting triangles. You will have 2 extra triangles. Save these for another project.
** Cut each square once diagonally for corner-setting triangles.

ADDITIONAL CUTTING FROM ASSORTED FABRICS

From each dark strip, cut:
- 2 squares, each 5¼" x 5¼"
- 1 square, 4½" x 4½"

From each medium 1 strip, cut:
- 4 squares, each 2½" x 2½"
- 1 square, 5¼" x 5¼"

From each medium 2 strip, cut:
- 2 rectangles, each 4½" x 5½"

BLOCK ASSEMBLY

Directions are for making 1 block. Repeat to make the required number of blocks for your quilt. For each block, choose one dark, one medium 1 fabric, and one medium 2 fabric.

1. Referring to "Making Quarter-Square Triangle Units" on page 14, place a 5¼" background square on top of a 5¼" dark square. Draw a diagonal line on the wrong side of the background square. Sew ¼" on each side of the diagonal line; cut on the drawn line. Repeat with a dark square and a medium 1 square.

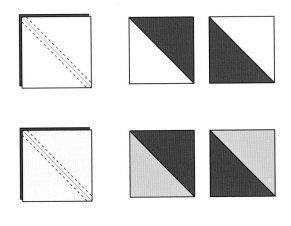

2. Place 2 bias squares right sides together (use one of each fabric combination made in step 1). Draw a diagonal line across the seam line on the wrong side of one of the bias square units. Sew ¼" from the diagonal line and cut on the line.

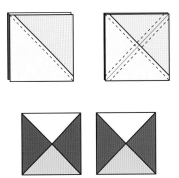

3. Sew a 2½" medium 1 square to one end of a 2½" x 3½" background rectangle. Sew 2 units together.

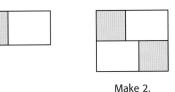

Make 2.

4. From template plastic, cut a 4½" square. Cut the square in half diagonally. Align the corner of the template with the pieced unit from step 3 and draw a line along the diagonal edge on the wrong side of the unit. Repeat on the opposite corner. Place the pieced unit right sides together with a medium 1 rectangle. Sew on both drawn lines, and cut between them to separate the units. Trim the seam allowances to ¼" if desired.

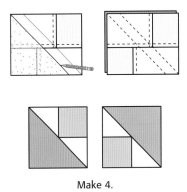

Make 4.

5. Sew the pieced units and the remaining dark square together to complete the block.

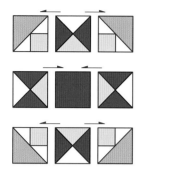

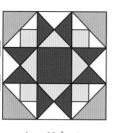

Lap: Make 8.
Twin: Make 18.
Queen: Make 32.

QUILT ASSEMBLY AND FINISHING

1. Referring to "Diagonally Set Quilts" on page 91, arrange and sew the blocks and side-setting triangles together into diagonal rows as shown in the quilt plan for your size quilt. Join the rows, adding the corner triangles last. Trim the edges of the quilt before adding borders.

Lap

Twin

Queen

2. Referring to the directions for piecing, measuring, and adding borders on page 92, add the 1½"-wide inner border, then the 4½"-wide outer border.

3. Layer the quilt top with backing and batting; baste.

4. Quilt as desired, or follow the quilting suggestion below.

5. Bind the edges and add a label.

CREATIVE OPTION

BARB EIKMEIER CUT all the parts for her blocks before she started assembling "Holiday Frenzy" on page 69. Then when she made the blocks, she purposefully did not match the center square to the star points.

Skyrocket

JELLY BEANS *by Sally Schneider, 2000, Breinigsville, Pennsylvania, 46" x 57". Bright pastels and a great print background make this quilt look like an Easter basket full of jelly beans. The Skyrocket pattern forms what looks like interlocking circles when the blocks are put together, even with sashing strips.*

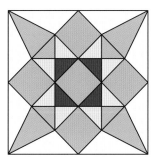

◄ NIGHTTIME SKYROCKETS *by Kari Lane, 2000, Lawson, Missouri, 46" x 57". Kari's varied navy backgrounds and jewel-colored prints work beautifully together in this stunning quilt. Kari favors jewel-toned prints and has a substantial collection of them.*

Finished Block Size: 10½"

MATERIALS
42"-wide fabric

	Crib	Twin	Queen
Finished Quilt Size	46" x 57½"	57½" x 69"	80½" x 92"
Assorted Light Prints	⅜ yd. total	½ yd. total	1 yd. total
Assorted Medium 1 Prints	¾ yd. total	1¼ yds. total	2½ yds. total
Assorted Medium 2 Prints	½ yd. total	½ yd. total	1⅛ yds. total
Assorted Dark Prints	⅝ yd.	1 yd.	2 yds.
Background *	1¼ yds.	1½ yds.	3 yds.
Inner Border	¼ yd.	⅜ yd.	½ yd.
Outer Border	¾ yd.	1 yd.	1¼ yds.
Backing	3 yds.	3¾ yds.	7¼ yds.
Batting	51" x 63"	63" x 75"	86" x 98"
Binding	½ yd.	⅝ yd.	¾ yd.

* You may choose just 1 fabric for the background, or choose several similar fabrics as Kari Lane did in "Nighttime Skyrockets" above.

CUTTING FOR CRIB SIZE

	No. of Strips	Strip Width	No. of Pieces	Piece Size
Background for Sashing	1	11"	31	1½" x 11"
Assorted Prints for Cornerstones			20	1½" x 1½"
Inner Border	5	1½"		
Outer Border	5	4½"		

CUTTING FOR TWIN SIZE

	No. of Strips	Strip Width	No. of Pieces	Piece Size
Background for Sashing	2	11"	49	1½" x 11"
Assorted Prints for Cornerstones			30	1½" x 1½"
Inner Border	6	1½"		
Outer Border	7	4½"		

CUTTING FOR QUEEN SIZE

	No. of Strips	Strip Width	No. of Pieces	Piece Size
Background for Sashing	3	11"	97	1½" x 11"
Assorted Prints for Cornerstones			56	1½" x 1½"
Inner Border	8	1½"		
Outer Border	8	4½"		

CUTTING FOR BLOCKS

CUTTING INSTRUCTIONS ARE for 1 block. Repeat for the required number of blocks for your quilt.

From one light print, cut:
- 2 squares, 3¾" x 3¾"

From one medium 1 print, cut:
- 1 strip, 3¾" x 21". From the strip, cut 1 square, 3¾" x 3¾", and 4 Template B pieces (page 79).

From one medium 2 print, cut:
- 1 square, 3¾" x 3¾"

From one dark print, cut:
- 5 squares, 3" x 3"

From the background fabric, cut:
- 1 strip, 2½" x 42". Fold the strip in half and cut 4 Template A pieces (page 79). Because you are cutting 2 pieces at a time from folded fabric, you will get 4 Template A pieces and 4 Template A reversed pieces. You can cut enough pieces for 2 blocks from one 42" strip.

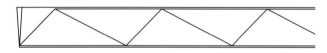

BLOCK ASSEMBLY

DIRECTIONS ARE FOR making 1 block. Repeat to make the required number of blocks for your quilt.

1. Referring to "Making Quarter-Square Triangle Units" on page 14, place a 3¾" light square on top of a 3¾" medium 1 square. Draw a diagonal line on the wrong side of the light square. Sew ¼" on each side of the diagonal line; cut on the drawn line. Repeat with a second light square and a medium 2 square.

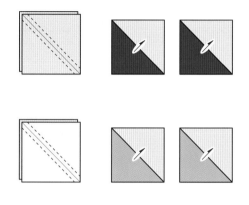

2. Place 1 bias square from each combination right sides together, with the light triangles on opposite sides. Draw a diagonal line across the seam line on the wrong side of 1 of the bias square units. Sew ¼" from the diagonal line and cut on the line. Repeat with the 2 remaining bias squares.

Make 4.

3. Sew together 4 quarter-square triangle units and five 3" dark squares to complete the Ohio Star unit.

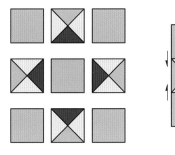 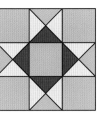 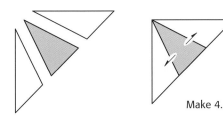

Crib: Make 12.
Twin: Make 20.
Queen: Make 42.

4. Sew a background piece A to one side of a medium 1 piece B; sew a piece A reversed to the opposite side to complete the corner unit.

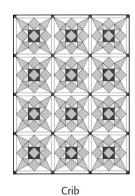

Make 4.

5. Sew a corner unit to each side of the Ohio Star unit, matching the seams. Sew 2 opposite sides first; then stitch the 2 remaining sides.

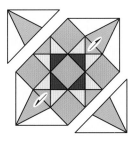 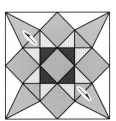

Crib: Make 12.
Twin: Make 20.
Queen: Make 42.

WHEN YOU *sew the triangle to the block, stitch with the triangle, which has a bias edge, on the bottom and the Ohio Star unit on top.*

QUILT ASSEMBLY AND FINISHING

1. Arrange the blocks, sashing strips (from background fabric), and cornerstones (from assorted prints) as shown in the quilt plan for your size quilt. Referring to "Quilts with Sashing" on page 90, sew the blocks and sashing strips together into horizontal rows. Sew the sashing strips and cornerstones together into horizontal rows. Join the rows, alternating rows of blocks with rows of sashing.

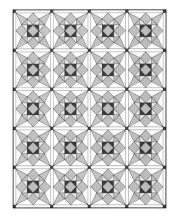

Crib

Twin

Queen

2. Referring to the directions for piecing, measuring, and adding borders on page 92, add the 1½"-wide inner border; then add the 4½"-wide outer border.

3. Layer the quilt top with backing and batting; baste.

4. Quilt as desired, or follow the quilting suggestion below.

5. Bind the edges and add a label.

CREATIVE OPTION

Try these pieced corner triangles with any 7½" block based on the nine-patch grid, such as Churn Dash.

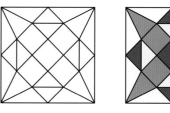

Churn Dash

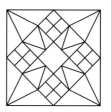
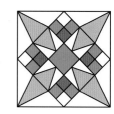

Fifty-Four Forty or Fight

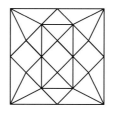
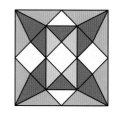

Split Nine Patch

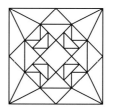
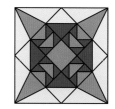

Capital T

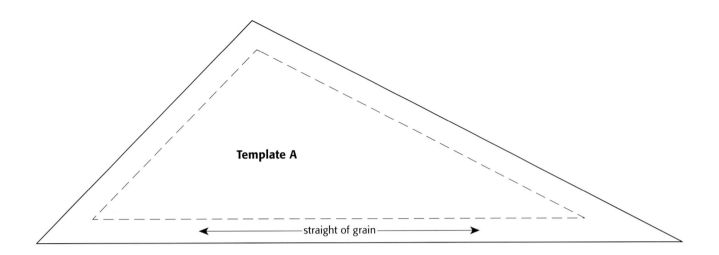

Template A

straight of grain

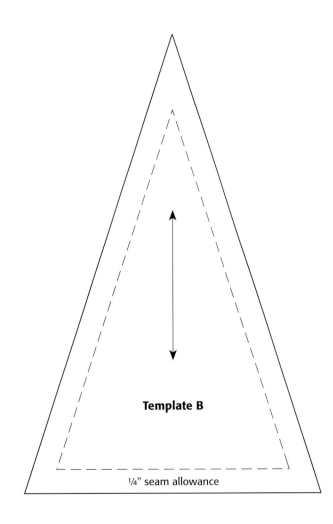

Template B

¼" seam allowance

Woven Star

WOVEN STAR *by Sally Schneider, 2000, Breinigsville, Pennsylvania, 65" x 80". Quilted by Kari Lane.*
An easy block, groups of three coordinated fabrics, and Ohio Star sashing strips combine for a stunning quilt, especially with
the black background. Choosing groups of three fabrics is the most fun; I kept wanting to do more.

Finished Block Size: 12"

MATERIALS

42"-wide fabric

	Lap	Twin	Queen
Finished Quilt Size	50½" x 65½"	65½" x 80½"	95½" x 95½"
Background	2¼ yds.	3¾ yd.	6⅜ yds.
Assorted Prints *	1½ yds. total	2⅞ yds. total	5½ yds. total
Inner Border	½ yd.	½ yd.	⅝ yd.
Outer Border	1 yd.	1⅛ yds.	1¼ yds.
Backing	3¼ yds.	4⅞ yds.	8½ yds.
Batting	56" x 71"	71" x 86"	101" x 101"
Binding	½ yd.	⅝ yd.	¾ yd.

* Select prints in groups of 3 fabrics that look good together. You will need a total of 12 different fabrics for the lap size, 20 for the twin size, and 39 for the queen size.

CUTTING FOR LAP SIZE

	No. of Strips	Strip Width	No. of Pieces	Piece Size
Background for Blocks	3	4½"	24	3½" x 4½"
	3	3½"	28	3½" x 3½" *
Assorted Prints for Blocks	2 each of 9	1½"		
Background for Sashing	3	4½"	24	4½" x 4½"
	2	6½"	17	3½" x 6½"
	1	12½"	10	3½" x 12½"
Each of 12 Prints for Sashing	1	4½"	2	4½" x 4½"
			1	3½" x 3½"
Inner Border	6	2"		
Outer Border	7	4½"		

CUTTING FOR TWIN SIZE

	No. of Strips	Strip Width	No. of Pieces	Piece Size
Background for Blocks	5	4½"	48	3½" x 4½"
	5	3½"	52	3½" x 3½" *
Assorted Prints for Blocks	2 each of 18	1½"		
Background for Sashing	5	4½"	40	4½" x 4½"
	3	6½"	31	3½" x 6½"
	2	12½"	14	3½" x 12½"
Each of 20 Prints for Sashing	1	4½"	2	4½" x 4½"
			1	3½" x 3½"
Inner Border	7	2"		
Outer Border	8	4½"		

* Reserve 4 squares for quilt assembly.

CUTTING FOR QUEEN SIZE

	No. of Strips	Strip Width	No. of Pieces	Piece Size
Background for Blocks	12	4½"	104	3½" x 4½"
	11	3½"	108	3½" x 3½" *
Assorted Prints for Blocks	2 each of 39	1½"		
Background for Sashing	9	4½"	72	4½" x 4½"
	5	6½"	60	3½" x 6½"
	2	12½"	20	3½" x 12½"
Each of 36 Prints for Sashing	1	4½"	2	4½" x 4½"
			1	3½" x 3½"
Inner Border	9	2"		
Outer Border	9	4½"		

* Reserve 4 squares for quilt assembly.

BLOCK ASSEMBLY

DIRECTIONS ARE FOR making 1 pair of blocks. Repeat to make remaining pairs required for your quilt.

1. Sew 1½"-wide strips of assorted prints together in groups of 3. Make 2 identical sets of strips. Crosscut the strip sets into a total of 8 segments, each 7½" wide.

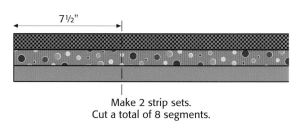

7½"

Make 2 strip sets.
Cut a total of 8 segments.

2. On the wrong side of the 3½" x 4½" background rectangles, draw 45° lines from both corners as shown using a Bias Square. Align the 45° line of a ruler with the side of the rectangle, making sure the edge of the ruler goes through the corner of the rectangle. Draw lines on half the rectangles in one direction; draw lines on the other half in the opposite direction.

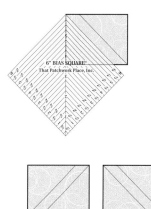

Lap: Make 12 of each.
Twin: Make 24 of each.
Queen: Make 54 of each.

3. Working with a group of 4 units from step 1 and 4 background rectangles with lines going in the same direction, place a background rectangle on one end of each striped rectangle. Make sure the stripes are always in the same direction. Sew on both lines. Cut between the 2 sewn lines.

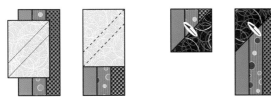

Make 4 of each.

4. Arrange the remaining 4 striped rectangles so that they face in the opposite direction (the stripes should be mirror images of the first group); then sew the background rectangles as in step 3.

Make 4 of each.

5. Sew one 3½" background square, 1 half-square triangle unit, and 1 rectangle unit together to make a quarter of a block. Be sure to orient the units as shown.

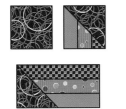

Make 4.

6. Sew 4 like quarter units together to complete each block. You will have 2 mirror-image blocks from each pair of strip sets.

NOTE: *You will have 1 extra block for the queen-size quilt.*

Make 1.

Make 1.

QUILT ASSEMBLY AND FINISHING

1. Referring to "Making Quarter-Square Triangle Units" on page 14, place a 4½" background square on top of a 4½" print square. Draw a diagonal line on the wrong side of the lighter square. Sew ¼" on each side of the diagonal line; cut on the drawn line. Repeat with a second background square and print square to make a second set of bias squares to match the first set.

Make 4.

2. Pair 2 bias squares right sides together with the light triangles on opposite sides. Draw a diagonal line across the seam line on the wrong side of 1 bias square unit. Sew ¼" from the diagonal line and cut on the line. Repeat with the remaining bias squares to make 4 matching quarter-square triangle units. Trim the resulting squares to 3½" x 3½".

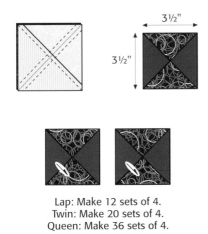

Lap: Make 12 sets of 4.
Twin: Make 20 sets of 4.
Queen: Make 36 sets of 4.

3. Arrange the blocks, quarter-triangle units, 3½" print squares, 3½" x 6½" and 3½" x 12½" background sashing strips, and 4½" background squares as shown in the quilt plan for your size quilt. Place the print squares in the centers of the Ohio Star units to match the adjacent quarter-square triangle units. Referring to "Quilts with Sashing" on page 90, sew the units together 1 row at time, keeping the colors in the same order in which you originally arranged them.

Lap

Twin

Queen

4. Referring to the directions for piecing, measuring, and adding borders on page 92, add the 2"-wide inner border; then add the 4½" wide outer border.

5. Layer the quilt top with backing and batting; baste.

6. Quilt as desired, or follow the quilting suggestion below.

7. Bind the edges and add a label.

Quartered Star

DANIEL'S BOON *by Deb Moffett-Hall, 2000, Hatfield, Pennsylvania, 38½" x 44". Deb's collection of homespun fabrics was the perfect starting place for this comforting small quilt for her son Danny. Using plaids for both the dark and light fabrics in this quilt would have blurred the lines of the design, so Deb chose tone-on-tone prints for the lights.*

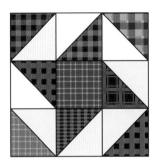

JUNGLE STARS *by Donna Lynn Thomas, 2000, Buckingham, Pennsylvania, 38" x 45". Quilted by Kari Lane. Hot, hot colors dispel the gloom of cold, rainy days in Donna's version of the Quartered Star pattern. She used the rainbow recipe method of choosing colors; each block is made with two fabrics, but no two fabrics are repeated. She chose prints based on the large floral border, selecting a few main color families from the print (color dots on the selvage help there) and then choosing different prints representing the different color families.*

Finished Block Size: 6"

MATERIALS
42"-wide fabric

	Crib	Lap	Twin	Queen
Finished Quilt Size	38½" x 44½"	44½" x 56½"	64½" x 82½"	82½" x 94½"
2¼" Light Bias Strips	40	64	144	224
2¼" Dark Bias Strips	40	64	144	224
or				
2" Finished Bias Squares *	240	384	864	1344
Assorted Dark Prints	¼ yd. total	⅜ yd. total	⅝ yd. total	⅞ yd. total
Inner Border	¼ yd.	⅜ yd.	⅜ yd.	½ yd.
Outer Border	½ yd.	⅝ yd.	1⅛ yds.	1⅜ yds.
Backing	1⅜ yds.	3 yds.	5 yds.	7½ yds.
Batting	44" x 50"	50" x 62"	70" x 88"	88" x 100"
Binding	⅜ yd.	½ yd.	⅝ yd.	¾ yd.

* As an alternative to making bias squares from the light and dark bias strips, you may use bias squares from your stash. For 2" finished bias squares, you will need 2½" unfinished bias squares.

CUTTING FOR CRIB SIZE

	No. of Strips	Strip Size	No. of Pieces	Piece Size
Assorted Dark Prints	4	2½" x 21"	30	2½" x 2½"
Inner Border	4	1½"		
Outer Border	4	3½"		

CUTTING FOR LAP SIZE

	No. of Strips	Strip Size	No. of Pieces	Piece Size
Assorted Dark Prints	6	2½" x 21"	48	2½" x 2½"
Inner Border	5	1½"		
Outer Border	5	3½"		

CUTTING FOR TWIN SIZE

	No. of Strips	Strip Size	No. of Pieces	Piece Size
Assorted Dark Prints	14	2½" x 21"	108	2½" x 2½"
Inner Border	7	1½"		
Outer Border	8	4½"		

CUTTING FOR QUEEN SIZE

	No. of Strips	Strip Size	No. of Pieces	Piece Size
Assorted Dark Prints	21	2½" x 21"	168	2½" x 2½"
Inner Border	9	1½"		
Outer Border	10	4½"		

BLOCK ASSEMBLY

1. Referring to "Making Bias Squares" on page 12, sew the 2¼"-wide light bias strips to the 2¼"-wide dark bias strips along both long edges. Press the strips to set the seams. Cut 2½" x 2½" bias squares from the sets.

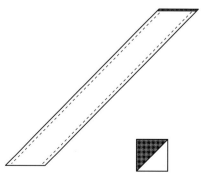

Crib: Cut 240.
Lap: Cut 384.
Twin: Cut 864.
Queen: Cut 1344.

2. Sew together 8 bias squares and 1 dark square to complete the block. You can use just 1 color for each block as in "Jungle Stars" on page 87, or mix them up as in "Daniel's Boon" on page 86.

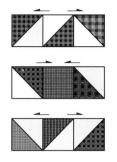
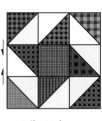

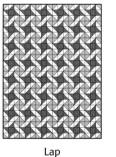

Crib: Make 30.
Lap: Make 48.
Twin: Make 108.
Queen: Make 168.

QUILT ASSEMBLY AND FINISHING

1. Arrange and sew the blocks together as shown in the quilt plan for your size quilt. Rotate the blocks as needed to ensure that adjacent seam allowances are pressed in opposite directions.

Crib

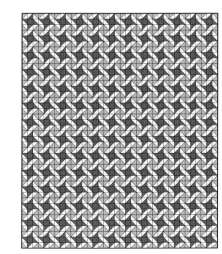

Lap

Twin

Queen

2. Referring to the directions for piecing, measuring, and adding borders on page 92, add the 1½"-wide inner border; then add the 3½"- or 4½"-wide outer border.

3. Layer the quilt top with backing and batting; baste.

4. Quilt as desired, or follow the quilting suggestion below.

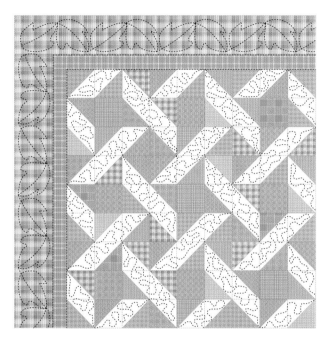

5. Bind the edges and add a label.

Quilt Assembly and Finishing

QUILTS WITH SASHING

MANY OF THE quilts in this book are assembled with sashing strips between the blocks. Some of them have pieced sashing strips that form stars when the strips are put together. All the quilts with sashing strips have corner squares, or cornerstones, where the strips meet.

1. To assemble a quilt with sashing strips, first arrange the blocks and sashing strips on a design wall or the floor. If the sashing strips have pieced units on the ends, arrange these to your liking. Assemble the sashing strips if necessary. To make sure the sashing strips stay in order, sew one at a time; when you have assembled it, return the strip to its place.

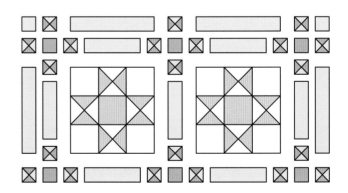

2. Once the sashing strips are assembled and arranged to your liking, pick up the top row of sashing strips and corner squares. Sew them together in order and press the seams toward the sashing strips. Return the row to its original position.

   NOTE: *If your quilt has pieced sashing strips, you will have two rows of sashing at the top and at the bottom of the quilt; these are required to complete the patterns in the sashing strips.*

3. Pick up the next row of blocks and sashing strips and sew them together in order. Press the seams toward the sashing strips. Return this row to its proper position.

4. Continue sewing rows of sashing strips and cornerstones and rows of sashing strips and blocks until they are all completed. Then sew the rows together in the proper order to complete the quilt top.

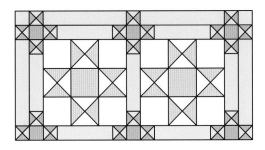

DIAGONALLY SET QUILTS

PIECING THE BLOCKS of a diagonally set quilt is no more difficult than piecing the blocks in a straight-set quilt. There are some tricks, however, that will make the job easy.

The spaces along the edge of a diagonally set quilt are filled with side-setting and corner-setting triangles. These triangles are cut so that the outside edge of the triangle is on the straight grain of the fabric. This makes it easier to attach borders or binding without stretching the quilt edges.

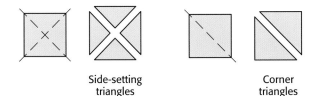

Side-setting triangles

Corner triangles

The directions for each quilt tell you how large to cut the triangles. They are intentionally cut larger than necessary and trimmed after the quilt top is completed.

Place these edge triangles in the spaces at the edge of your quilt; then piece them to the ends of the blocks as you sew the rows together. Follow the quilt plan for your particular quilt.

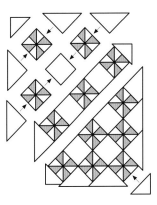

Notice that the right-angle points of the triangles are kept on the same line as the block edges, and the sharper points of the triangles extend beyond the edge the block. Because it is essential to keep the long edge straight, you must trim the triangle points off. Lay your ruler across the top of the blocks, keeping the edge of the ruler even with the raw edge of the block. Trim the triangles even with the raw edge.

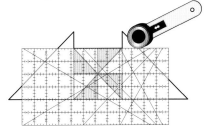

Once the quilt top is completed, square up the edges of the quilt, leaving a ¼"-wide seam allowance all around.

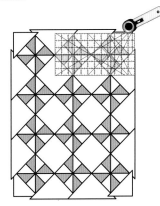

NOTE: *Until a diagonally set quilt is layered and basted for quilting, it is extremely important to use care when handling it. The vertical and horizontal planes of these quilts are on the bias and will stretch very easily. While basting, pat the quilt flat rather than push fullness to one edge or the other. And be careful not to stretch or distort the unquilted or unbasted top when folding it. You may stretch the center of the quilt so much that it will never lie flat again.*

BORDERS WITH STRAIGHT-CUT CORNERS

I PREFER TO cut border strips across the width of the fabric and join them end to end as needed. Less fabric is required when borders are cut this way.

To keep your quilt square, it is essential to cut the border strips to fit before you add them to the quilt top. But it's not necessary to measure borders with a tape measure. You only need to lay the strips across the center of the quilt and trim them even with the edges.

1. To measure borders, lay 2 strips across the center of the quilt lengthwise. Trim both ends even with the raw edge of the quilt. Fold border strips in half and in quarters and mark the positions. Mark the same positions on both long edges of the quilt.

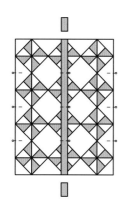

2. Pin borders to the quilt, matching the markings. Pin about every 3" along the border, easing if necessary. Stitch the border strips to the quilt.

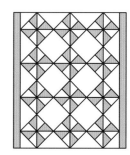

3. Repeat this procedure for the width of the quilt.

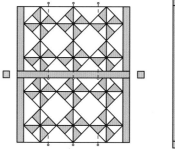

BORDERS WITH CORNER SQUARES

1. If your borders have corner squares, measure and cut border strips for all 4 sides before you sew them to the quilt.

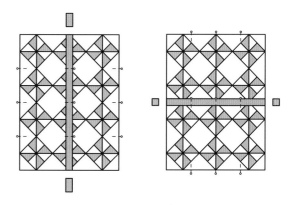

2. Pin and stitch the side borders as directed for straight-cut borders. Sew a corner square to each end of the top and bottom border, then attach it to the quilt.

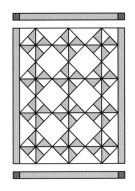

QUILT BACKS

I FIND THAT running the seam lengthwise on a pieced backing often requires more fabric than is necessary. Instead, I prefer to calculate the yardage required for quilt backs to allow the least amount of excess fabric. (Notice that I do not use the word "waste." All excess fabric from the backs of my quilts becomes strips, bias squares, or pieces for the front of other quilts. Nothing is wasted!)

For all quilts up to 75" long, I piece the backing with 1 crosswise seam in the center. Measure the width of the quilt, add 6", and double this measurement; divide by 36 to calculate yards of backing to purchase.

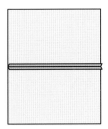

For quilts that are longer than 75" and up to 75" wide, I piece the backing with 1 lengthwise seam in the center. Measure the length of the quilt, add 6", and double this measurement; divide by 36 to calculate yards.

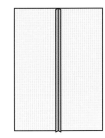

I piece backings for quilts even larger than this with three lengths of fabric. Measure the shortest side of the quilt, add 6", triple this measurement; divide by 36 to calculate yards.

After the backing is pieced, press it to remove all wrinkles and fold lines, and to make sure all the seams are flat. Press seams open.

BASTING

BASTE YOUR QUILT on a large dining room table, Ping-Pong table, or on several banquet tables pushed together. Sometimes you can use the tables at quilt shops when they are not holding classes. I baste my quilts in the fellowship hall at my church.

Unfold your batting the day before you plan to baste the quilt to let it rest and to get some of the wrinkles out, or place it in the dryer on air dry for about 20 minutes.

1. Lay the pressed quilt back on the table, wrong side up, and secure the edges to the table. Use masking tape or binder clips. Lay the batting on top, centering it on the backing.

2. Place the quilt top on the batting, centering it and making sure there is about 3" of extra batting and backing all around the edges. Smooth the quilt, being careful not to stretch it. Keep all borders and sashings as straight as possible.

3. To thread baste, sew a grid of large stitches, starting in the middle of the quilt. Stitch about every 6", parallel with the edges of the quilt. If the quilt is set diagonally, stitch the grid parallel with the seams. Stitch around the edges last, folding the backing over the front of the quilt to encase the batting. Use the thread-baste method for hand quilting.

4. You can also use safety pins. Layer the backing, batting, and quilt top as you did in steps 1 and 2; then place safety pins about 3" to 4" apart. Use size 2 safety pins; these are large enough to hold all 3 layers, but they won't leave big holes in the quilt. Use safety pins for machine quilting.

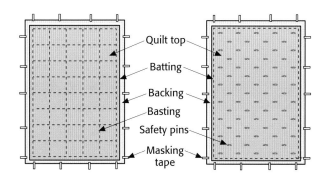

5. If you have a quilt-tack tool, you can use it to baste your quilts for either hand quilting or machine quilting. It is a fast method and it holds the layers securely. The tabs of the tacks

are all on top of the quilt and are easy to remove if they get in the way of the needle.

Quilt tacks

BINDING

I CUT STRAIGHT-GRAIN strips, 2¼" wide, across the full width of the fabric.

1. Sew the strips together to make 1 long strip; press seam allowances open.

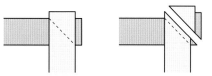

2. Press the strip in half lengthwise, wrong sides together.

3. Trim excess backing and batting. Place the edge of the binding on the right side of the quilt about 15" from a corner; the raw edges should be even. Leaving about a 6" tail and using a ⅜" seam allowance, stitch the binding to the quilt. End and backstitch ⅜" from the corner.

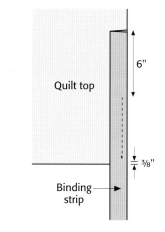

4. To miter the corner, fold the binding strip at a 45° angle away from the quilt. Then fold the binding strip back on itself, parallel with the next edge of the quilt.

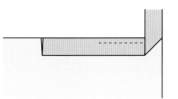

5. Stitch, beginning ⅜" from the edge of the fabric; continue to the next corner. Repeat the steps above for each corner, leaving a 6" tail at the end of the binding strip.

6. Fold the unstitched binding edges back on themselves so they just meet in the middle over the unsewn area of the quilt top. Press the fold.

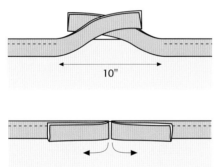

10"

7. Unfold both sides of the binding and match the centers of the pressed **X**s. The right end should be on top of the left. Draw a diagonal line from the upper left corner to the lower right. Pin and stitch.

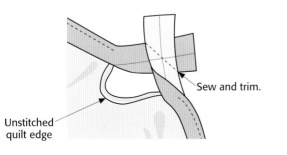

Sew and trim.

Unstitched quilt edge

8. Trim the edges and press the seam open. Refold the binding, pressing the fold, and stitch the remainder of the binding.

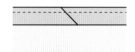

9. Fold the binding over and blind stitch on the wrong side. The folded edge of the binding should cover the machine stitched line on the back. Stitch the miter that forms at each corner.

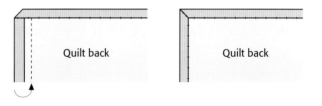

Quilt back   Quilt back

LABELS

ALWAYS ADD A label to your quilt. Years from now, your family will want to know who made the quilt and when it was made. The label should include at least your name, your town, and the year the quilt was made.

You can write the information on a piece of muslin with a permanent marker and stitch it to the quilt, or you can make a fancier label using templates available in a variety of books and using colored permanent markers. There are even labels available as fabric yardage. If your sewing machine does lettering, you can make a label that way.

Stitch the label to the back of the quilt.

About the Author

SALLY grew up in northeastern Pennsylvania, the daughter of an accomplished seamstress who taught her to sew when she was only eight years old. She became a nurse, but never lost her interest in needlework. When she moved to Europe with her family in the 1970s, she discovered quiltmaking, a hobby that offered a challenge uniquely suited to her talents and her desire to create something both practical and beautiful. The first quilt Sally made was a scrap quilt. Since that time, she has pieced more than 250 quilts (and quilted about 175 of them). Quiltmaking has become her profession. She has taught classes and lectured throughout the United States and in Canada. She is the author of three other books, including *ScrapMania: More Quick-Pieced Scrap Quilts*. She co-authored *Traditional Quilts with Painless Borders* with Barbara J. Eikmeier. All of Sally's books were published by Martingale & Company.

Sally lives in Allentown, Pennsylvania, at the edge of Pennsylvania Dutch country, with her dog, Merlin. Now that her children are all grown and have moved to all parts of the country, she loves traveling to visit them (especially her grandson in Texas!). Sally is an active member of the Keystone Quilters Guild in Quakertown, Pennsylvania.